AF646967

LEAN, MEAN AND PROFITABLE

LEAN, MEAN AND PROFITABLE

Success Stories of Self-made Indian Entrepreneurs

Diksha Dutta

Foreword
by
Sanjeev Bikhchandani

BLOOMSBURY
NEW DELHI • LONDON • OXFORD • NEW YORK • SYDNEY

BLOOMSBURY INDIA
Bloomsbury Publishing India Pvt. Ltd
Second Floor, LSC Building No. 4, DDA Complex, Pocket C – 6 & 7,
Vasant Kunj, New Delhi 110070

BLOOMSBURY, BLOOMSBURY INDIA and the Diana logo
are trademarks of Bloomsbury Publishing Plc

First published in India 2023
This edition published 2023

Copyright © Diksha Dutta, 2023

Diksha Dutta has asserted her right under the Indian Copyright Act to be identified as the author of this work

All rights reserved. No part of this publication may be reproduced or transmitted in any form or by any means, electronic or mechanical, including photocopying, recording or any information storage or retrieval system, without the prior permission in writing from the publishers

The instant work contains excerpts of personal interviews conducted by the author between 2016 and 2021, the contents of which are reproduced with the consent of the interviewees. The views expressed are those of the interviewees alone and do not reflect the opinions or positions of Bloomsbury Publishing India Pvt. Ltd

This book is solely the responsibility of the author and the publisher has had no role in the creation of the content and does not have responsibility for anything defamatory or libellous or objectionable

Bloomsbury Publishing Plc does not have any control over, or responsibility for, any third-party websites referred to or in this book. All internet addresses given in this book were correct at the time of going to press. The author and publisher regret any inconvenience caused if addresses have changed or sites have ceased to exist, but can accept no responsibility for any such changes

ISBN: PB: 978-93-87146-97-6; e-ISBN: 978-93-87146-98-3
2 4 6 8 10 9 7 5 3 1

Typeset in Fournier MT Std by Manipal Technologies Limited
Printed and bound in India by Thomson Press India Ltd

FSC www.fsc.org MIX Paper from responsible sources FSC® C010615

To find out more about our authors and books visit www.bloomsbury.com and sign up for our newsletters

To my friend Angela, who changed my life unknowingly

CONTENTS

AUTHOR'S NOTE

What makes a story worth telling? This is one of the most common questions in the media and newsrooms. And in the world of business reporting, it often boils down to numbers. The higher the millions attached to your story, the more likely it is to hit page one or get space in the next edition. The higher the stakes, the more respected you are as a journalist among your peers. But those were never the reasons why I became a journalist or chose it as my first profession. My passion lies in writing stories that can be genuinely helpful, whether to businesses or consumers, regardless of the numbers attached to them. I am drawn to dark horses in the game of start-ups.

For me, stories become truly interesting when they forge their own path. They become worth telling because the people behind them are heroes. It is not for us in the media to define who these heroes are. This book aims to shed light on the stories of founders who started in obscurity at a time when VC money wasn't easily accessible and bootstrapping wasn't celebrated. Through my interviews with different founders, I strive to reveal the common decisions that can often go wrong on the start-up journey.

Indian entrepreneurs often compare themselves to global start-ups and seek to learn from their operations. However, this comparison is like equating apples to oranges since Indian consumers and socioeconomic conditions are unique. This book delves into the choices made by self-funded businesses to attract more customers by understanding different pricing strategies, global aspirations and the challenges of employee retention. It also explores how funded, successful businesses have achieved their goals. Offering a wealth of choices and techniques, this book provides valuable advice to businesses seeking growth and success, enabling them to select strategies that best suit their needs.

This book could not have been completed without the invaluable guidance of Mr Sanjeev Bikhchandani, who inspired me to delve into this topic. I am grateful to my friends and acquaintances – Nikita Rana, Nimish Sawant, Tina Nayak, Sandeep Singh, Miguel Encarnacion and Angela De Giacomo – who read the manuscript and provided constructive feedback to enhance the quality of the book. My husband and mother gave me immense moral support to complete this book in situations when it had taken a back seat, and my best friend Sanjna never let me forget that this was something I needed to complete for myself. Lastly, I express deep gratitude to Bloomsbury Publishing India and the entire team who helped turn this dream into reality.

FOREWORD

The customer's money is better than the investor's. This statement stands true since the day I started my journey as a founder in 1990. The reason is simple. If you're getting the customer's money and getting it repeatedly, you probably have a viable business, and so the investor's money will follow. The other way around doesn't always work out.

When I started Naukri.com in 1997, my only aim was to break even. This was a time when there were only fourteen thousand internet accounts in India. Around 1999, we started getting calls from investors, which I found amusing. Why would people want to give me money for my company? At the time, we were doing ₹36 lakh (approx $84,000) in annual revenue, and one young non-resident Indian (NRI) wanted to invest $2 million in the company. I walked away as the concept of raising capital was very new then – not only for me but for the start-up industry. However, we raised money later when we were ready and then got publicly listed. Today, because of the core business and our investments in companies such as Zomato, Info Edge is valued at over $5 billion. But the focus throughout has been on solving an unsolved problem and keeping the customer at the centre of all decisions. Now, even though I don't run Info Edge on a day-to-day basis, when we're looking for companies to invest in, it is these basic traits that we look for in the founders: they should have the tenacity to persist, have a high degree of integrity and be able to feel the pulse of their consumers.

It must be far more tempting for entrepreneurs today to raise venture capital (VC) money, but in a market like India, customer understanding is far more critical.

India already has over fifty-thousand start-ups with two to three being born daily.[1] Young India is inspired to launch their companies and eventually list them publicly. Whether it is Deepinder Goyal, the founder of Zomato, or Yashish Dahiya, who co-founded Policybazaar, these are stories of individuals from middle-class backgrounds with no business families to back them. They've built these humungous companies and then listed them publicly. They're now the poster boys of the Indian start-up ecosystem because they probably inspired hundreds of millions of people in India. And if a hundred million people are inspired, maybe ten million will try to do something about it, among which maybe one million start-ups will emerge.

With enormous VC funds coming to India and ninety unicorns later, and while the way we fund our start-ups or run our companies may have changed, the fundamentals of doing business remain the same. Are you solving a real problem? Will you be able to get traction without marketing? What's your business model? These are very simple questions, but I often see young founders struggling with answers that are backed with facts.

If you're an entrepreneur and want to give India its next Zomato-sized company, dream big but start small. That is what this book is about. It's about the nitty-gritty of getting the basics right: customer understanding, product, pricing and revenue generation. The detailed experiences of entrepreneurs who've become unicorns and remained bootstrapped encapsulate essential learning on how start-ups discover their customers and how they pivot when they need to. Funding or no funding, your customers should always be your focus, not how to raise the next round of funding.

There is much to be learned from those who've gone down the path of entrepreneurship before us. So many critical decisions need to be taken when starting out: the place of incorporation, the pace of growth, the size of the team, the source of funds and handling the day-to-day challenges of running a business. Having an authentic guide in the form of a book that explains how it's all been done before is extremely valuable.

I first met Diksha in 2012, when she was a journalist at the *Financial Express*, and have tracked her journey since she moved from being a start-up journalist in India to now working with start-ups across the globe. Her fascination with start-up founders' journeys has been inspiring, and I often recall her as someone who asks the right and the difficult questions. I am positive this book will give you answers to these questions and inspire people across the globe to work with Indian start-up founders.

Sanjeev Bikhchandani
Founder, Info Edge

I

Do Start-ups Need Just Money or VC Money?

I can feel the difference in the air. Within five minutes of entering a start-up's office, I know if it is funded by a VC firm or built brick by brick with its own funding, which means lesser money and a shoestring budget. The latter has always fascinated me more than the former. From posters on the walls and office spaces where employees sit to even corridors and washrooms, everything reflects whether it is the ostentatious spending of VC money or the sweat and struggle of getting returns on one's own investments. Don't be misled; this is not a book that thrashes VC-backed businesses but one that respects self-funded businesses. It also studies successfully funded businesses – the ones who sustained and bootstrapped themselves for a long time before raising capital.

What a fascinating story it becomes when the prey becomes the predator. The investor chases the start-up. It might seem far-fetched to you, but it is possible, and it happens. The chase reminds me of what Warren Buffet once said: 'Games are won by players who focus on the playing field not by those whose eyes are glued to the scoreboard.'[1] An entrepreneur's playing field is their business and that is where their focus is expected to be. Capital is necessary to build a business but excess capital at an early stage has the potential to drive an entrepreneur to splurge.

Bhanu Chopra, the founder of RateGain, a software-as-a-service (SaaS) company that raised capital after five years of being bootstrapped, said, 'Earlier, we had just one office abroad. After funding, we had six. When you are bootstrapped, you implement one out of ten ideas you have, but when funded, you can take more risks and implement all of them together. Speed is everything.' SaaS is a subscription-based cloud-computing service that gives customers access to applications through the internet.

Sometimes ideas work and sometimes they don't. There is a fine line between investing wisely and investing blindly to scale up. This book will talk about ideas that have worked for businesses and have been a success. To reiterate, this is a book of ideas that have been a success, not of entrepreneurs. What does success mean to you as an entrepreneur, I have no idea. But I can definitely claim that I have a fair idea of what a successful business is.

Success can mean different things to different entrepreneurs. For some, having a single-digit stake in the company they founded and owning a yacht by selling that stake is a success. For another, building and selling one company after another is a success. There are also people for whom it's important to stick to an organisation until they take control of all decisions. However, if this book helps even one entrepreneur make the right decision for their start-up, it will be considered a success. In reality, though, it is a challenge to measure and define entrepreneurial success and give it a clear definition. There is however a clear definition of a business that is *not* a success. A business that is not making any profit is definitely not successful. Similarly, if one cannot assess or predict when a business will start making profits, it cannot be considered a successful business. There are exceptions to this rule when one looks at business-to-consumer (B2C) players such as Flipkart and Paytm. They were yet to make any profit in 2022, but they both attracted immense VC money, with Flipkart even getting bought off by the US retail giant Walmart. According to the media, these two companies can be called a success.

The most important responsibility of a business is to create value for its users and make money for its investors. While an entrepreneur can afford to focus only on the top line, a business has to worry about the bottom line at the end of the day. A business will struggle without the bottom line, eventually dying in the arms of the investor who clings on to that top-heavy business till its last breath. This means that an entrepreneur can be successful in an unsuccessful business.

What definition of success you choose as an entrepreneur is your personal one. For this book, I met more than fifty entrepreneurs. More importantly, I tried to analyse how they relate to the definition of a successful business. It is not often that you meet a young entrepreneur such as Paras Chopra, the founder of Wingify, who chooses not to raise external capital. 'We want to take Wingify where it is much stronger than just taking money and doing a short sprint with it,' he said. 'We prefer running a marathon to a short sprint.' Formula-based growth can't prove to be a success in his definition.

He looks to the future with hope and a sense of idealism. 'Our dream is to build Wingify into an institution rather than grow fast, have an IPO and then have materialistic possessions,' he said. 'Then what? We feel there is a charm in building an institution rather than growing very fast – making a five-year plan of expected growth and reaching a valuation.' I am so glad that he was the first person I interviewed for this book in 2016. It was like a reaffirmation that one must write about entrepreneurs like him who are a breath of fresh air in today's time when everyone is chasing investors. On average, I meet three new start-ups every week for detailed conversations on their venture, and it is seldom that the topic of raising capital does not come up. On the contrary, Wingify, founded in 2009, began as a start-up providing A/B testing and did not raise any external capital. It was done by choice, not by chance.

If one studies the growth of companies such as Wingify, the definition of success takes a different turn. The fact that Wingify did not raise external capital did not kill the company's desire to scale up to become a unicorn. In June 2016, Chopra wrote in his personal blog,

> Last month at Wingify, we hit a million dollars of recurring revenue. I'm very happy that the team has been able to achieve this milestone, especially because we're entirely bootstrapped and haven't raised any outside investment. There has been a lot of enthusiasm about the million-dollar-a-month figure, and all Wingifighters are pumped up to convert the 'm' into a 'b'.[2]

As of 2020, Wingify had close to $23 million annual recurring revenue with over two hundred and fifty team members from diverse revenue streams. And it's still bootstrapped!

As an entrepreneur, if you are spending a quarter or more of your time a month chasing funding for your business, take a deep breath and rethink your priorities and goals.

In 2022, as this book was being edited, I had the chance to meet a founder such as Karthik Sridharan, who is convinced that he will go the bootstrapped way to build his start-up Flexiple, a global network of freelance developers and designers. When I asked him what makes him so sure of not wanting to raise capital, he said it's not that his thinking has evolved over the years; he always thought of funding and VCs as one of the many tools that a start-up has. One should look at funding as one would, for example, search engine optimisation (SEO), which is also just a tool.

Sridharan said,

> You need to ask yourself whether you need that particular tool or not. At any point in time, the moment we feel that the only deterrent factor to our growth is the fact that we don't have external funding, we will definitely go for it. Because, at the end of the day, all that every start-up should be optimising for is success. There is no hard and fast rule that a tech start-up that's not funded is inferior to a VC-funded start-up. Those are just random notions.

You need to go back to the drawing board and ask yourself the fundamental question: what is going to make my start-up successful? 'The day we feel that funding is the only reason that my start-up isn't able to find the next level of success, we will definitely explore that option,' Sridharan said.

Turakhia and Kamath Brothers: In for the Long-Term Game

There are many examples of successful businesses with zero external capital. In December 2016, I met Divyank Turakhia, who had sold his advertising technology firm, Media.net, for $900 million in the August of that year. Media.net was a subsidiary of the Directi group, which Divyank ran with his brother Bhavin. The company did not raise any external capital since its inception in 2000. This means that the Turakhia brothers were the sole claimants to the exit value of $900 million. Divyank had visited India for a couple of days to speak at the TiE Global Summit 2016 when he squeezed in some time for an interview with me before his flight to California. His panel discussion was a full house on a late Sunday afternoon. It was surprising to see an audience who wanted to know about this thirty-four-year-old entrepreneur who made a successful exit from an ad-tech company with zero VC funding by selling it to a Chinese consortium. I was curious too and wanted to know why and how he flew 'solo' for so long. He told me that venture capitalists approached him all the time, but not once did he go hunting for one.

Investors were keen on investing in Media.net as it was a profit-making venture from the beginning and had the capabilities to scale up. Professionally or personally, anything that is easily available does not excite us much, and maybe that is what made the Turakhia brothers bootstrap their start-up. While talking to him, he exuded a sense of confidence that could make others a little uncomfortable. 'We did not need the money and hence did not choose to raise it,' he told me. 'Whatever we were doing, it was working well, and we were so busy doing it that we could not deviate. If we saw there was a benefit, we could have done it.' His clarity and confidence are inspiring. On 16 October 2018, he wrote to the Media.net staff, telling them that he would be stepping down as the CEO to focus his energies on his global investment portfolios:[3]

> It has been about eight years since I founded Media.net as a bootstrapped startup. As you know, about two years ago we sold it to Shuzhi (formerly known as Miteno) in a transaction valued at $900 million, one of the largest ad tech exits ever. We have continued to grow consistently since the sale. We are one of the top 5 largest online advertising businesses worldwide by market cap. We have recently crossed 1300 employees worldwide vs 800 in 2016... Yes, you have seen great success and have had an incredible journey thus far. But your historic performance should not mean that you slow down in any way. In our industry, only the most innovative companies will thrive. The rest will disappear. To stay relevant, you must continue to

> build revolutionary products and not get comfortable. We are always in version 1.0 for everything. Everything that we see around—is, can and will be—a lot more efficient in another 5-10-20-50-100 years. Hence, never believe everything is already done—'cause nothing is ever done. One of our biggest market advantages has been that good software isn't written in months. Building a large scaleable platform such as ours takes years of investment and hundreds of employees. Many companies will have the money to invest and can recruit great talent, but they will still need to spend years to create what *you* have today. That is our *biggest* moat! Keep building on it and do not let it shrink in size. When there is volatility and turmoil (and there always will be time and time again), *don't* get greedy and try to manage for a specific financial quarter or year. Our margins have always been normalised, even where we could have dialled this up. Normalised and transparent margins make it extremely hard for any competitor to cut you on price. Always run the business for the long term.

Another example of a business that did not raise capital is Zerodha, a Bangalore-based online stock trading B2C company. Nithin Kamath, the company's CEO, tells me that when he was initially seeking capital, it was not available, but later it seemed like a blessing in disguise:

> When we started, VCs were not looking at the brokerage industry or online trading companies, and the VC industry was not big. Fintech in India had not evolved by then. I met a few investors and tried to understand if external capital could help our company. I still think if we would have got funding, we would not have been able to grow the way we are growing today. I can understand the pulse of the brokerage and trading market better than VCs. We have been able to take many decisions swiftly without institutional investors on board, and we continue to do so now.

As of 2023, Zerodha had eight million users.[4] It's rare for a non-VC-funded start-up, especially in a stockbrokerage space, to post profits.

Why would you not raise capital when a VC is desperate to give it to you? The concept of running your company with someone else's capital sounds fancy to many start-ups today, at least to 90 per cent of the start-ups I meet. So what stopped entrepreneurs such as the Turakhias and the Kamaths from raising capital?

Divyank said this is the question that often start-ups don't ask themselves. 'We often asked ourselves that if we raised $20 million, could we grow at 5x?' he said. 'Whenever we did this math, we realised that we could reach the growth of 20x even without capital. Unless there is a strategic benefit in addition to money, it made no sense for us to raise capital.'

I have given examples of two companies that are thriving without VC money. It is often thought that business-to-business (B2B) companies can survive easily with less capital, which is true. However, the example of Infibeam, an e-commerce company that got a public listing with zero funding, stunned me in 2016. The company continues to run a B2C e-commerce model smartly with the money it gets from its B2B business. How did they do it? What model did they use? More on this later.

In their early days, many journalists did not know about these businesses because the founders were too busy on the playing field that they forgot to come out and talk about themselves and their businesses. This book will unravel the stories of these businesses from scratch. (The chapters will deal with all the facets of running a successful business and how the founders of these businesses did it – step by step from conception, pricing and first few customers to scaling up.)

Venture Capital Funding Is Beyond Just Getting Moolah for Your Start-up

The stories of the journey of raising capital through VC and private equity (PE) funding are not always glorious and smooth even if the investors show keen interest. I have been a witness to the ugliest ones. While PE and VC funding amounts and types vary, the level of drama is the same. PE[5] is sometimes confused with VC[6] because both refer to firms that invest in and exit from companies by selling their investments in equity financing by holding initial public offerings (IPOs)[7]. However, there are significant differences in the way firms involved in the two types of funding conduct business. PE and VC buy different types and sizes of companies, invest different amounts of money and claim different percentages of equity in the companies

FIG 1.1 The difference between private equity and venture capital

	PE	VC
Stage of Company	✓ Later stage, established ✓ 5+ years of operating history ✓ EBITDA positive	✓ Start-up or early stage ✓ <5 years of history ✓ Pre-EBITDA
Valuation Methodology	✓ Multiple of EBITDA	✓ Multiple of Revenue ✓ Other, Multiple of "Dreams"
Amount of Capital Invested per Deal / # of Investments Made	✓ 10 or fewer investments per fund ✓ More concentrated portfolio	✓ 20–40+ investments per fund ✓ Less concentrated portfolio
Ownership Position Taken	✓ Control, 51–100%	✓ Non-control, <50%
Exit Strategies	✓ Other PE funds ✓ Strategic buyers	✓ IPO ✓ PE funds ✓ Strategic buyers
Returns Expectations	✓ 2-3× invested capital per deal	✓ 3×+ plus total return for the fund ✓ Will lose money on serveral deals ✓ 80% of returns from 20% of deals
Team Backgrounds	✓ Investment banking ✓ Management consulting ✓ Operations (less common)	✓ Operations ✓ Enterpreneurs ✓ Investment banking ✓ Management consulting

Source: ClearLights Partners[8]

they invest in. PE is capital invested in a company or other entity that is not publicly listed or traded. VC on the other hand is funding given to start-ups or other young businesses that show potential for long-term growth.

Remember the north Indian kidswear apparel brand Lilliput? Parents of the late 1990s must have heard about it. In 2012 I started hardcore reporting on PE and VC deals; it was a bad time for the retail industry. Investors, both institutional and VC, were not very open to investing in any brick-and-mortar retail business then.

The reason was simple. Lilliput had then settled a legal tussle with its global PE investors, Texas Pacific Group (TPG) and Bain Capital, which reportedly ended with one of the biggest write-downs by a PE investor in India. When I spoke with analysts in the sector, I realised what kinds of disasters befall an organisation if there are irregularities in management and how ugly stories can be if companies raise capital when they are not ready for funding. The point here is that while capital is necessary for businesses to grow, one must do due diligence on whether the company is ready to raise it.

The scale of the company or the number of employees are not the parameters that should make you decide whether you are set to raise capital. The most important thing is that your company must yield phenomenal returns to the investor in the most efficient way. Be prepared to invest a lot of time in corporate governance once you have an investor on board. It is someone else's money that you are dealing with, and they will need proof of concept at each step of scaling up.

Once a start-up has investors on board, a lot of time goes into corporate governance. It is important to prioritise things. Spend less time caring about customised office merchandise, which media has covered your start-up, the list of holidays for employees or even the number of senior people in the organisation. In the early days, you just need to focus on working and getting business.

Corporate governance is necessary, but it will anyway come with time when you expand.

'Once you grow, you do need that corporate governance anyway. This happens with hiring the right people. Now we will go public, and it will help corporate governance. I don't think that was our focus in the early days,' said Divyank in an interview in 2016 when Media.net was preparing to go public.

Are VCs or PEs the Best Choice for Your Business?

For a journalist, chasing the closure of a PE or a VC deal is no less edgy than trying to predict the climax of a Jefferey Archer novel. A breakup between an investor and entrepreneur hurt the journalist who broke the story of their initial 'hook-up' as much as the two parties involved. The story of Asif Merchant, the CEO of Catwalk, a Mumbai-headquartered shoe retail company, is one of my favourites. It taught me a lot about deal reporting and Merchant about closing a funding deal. During the time when I was covering deals in the consumer segment, I was also tracking Catwalk because it was in the middle of raising capital. It had signed a few term sheets and had immense investor interest. I tracked Merchant down at a conference at Vivanta Surajkund where he was speaking on a panel on the retail sector. I wanted to know whether India Value Fund Advisors (IVFA) was investing $18 million in Catwalk as was the rumour then reported by a fellow journalist from another media publication.[9] Those days, I mostly wrote about who is investing in whom and what, and who has pulled money out of which company. As soon as Merchant finished his talk, I approached him for an interview request and realised that he was as keen to talk to me as I was and invited me for lunch in the cafeteria of the hotel.

'The deal is not happening,' he said, and I could sense that he wanted me to write about it. He wanted me to write his version of the breakup – yet another breakup of a deal that was leaked to a journalist. He had numerous learnings from this breakup and most importantly understood how investors work.

Here is what happened: In February 2013, after interviewing Merchant I wrote about how Catwalk is not raising capital from IVFA and the details of the breakup. Basically, it was not a good match in terms of expectations from both sides. In March 2014, I again reported that Merchant is back in the game and looking for funding. This time, he told me, he was looking for a strategic investor not just VC or PE money – someone who could add value than just capital. He had understood by then that he needed an investor who appreciated the brick-and-mortar retail business.[10] In 2016, the media reported the consummation of a deal between Catwalk and a strategic investor. The name of the investor was not revealed, only that it was an international footwear brand, not a PE or VC fund. I called him to congratulate him and he confirmed the deal. By 2016, I had quit full-time journalism – deal reporting was not my claim to fame any more.

Between 2013 and 2016 when Merchant could not find a suitable investor, he found creative ways to survive without external capital. He needed capital but looked for various other alternatives to scale up his retail brand. He just needed money, not particularly PE or VC money. This is the case with all entrepreneurs who think they cannot survive without capital from VC investors.

'In early 2010, our balance sheets and working capital told us that we are heading towards a scenario when there will be no returns, and it can be sorted only when we have a good debt-to-equity ratio. We needed funds,' Merchant told me over a phone call in 2017. 'By 2012, we had three consecutive negative balance sheets. We had PwC as our auditors.' By 2013, getting a VC was the only viable option for Merchant, but he gradually realised that fundraising is an ongoing process and there is no timeline to it. His business cannot stop – all his energy cannot go into raising capital and that in any case cannot be the only rescue. There should always be a plan B to fall back on. This is what entrepreneurs do not realise these days. Businesses that are dependent only on external funding will eventually face an existential crisis.

Merchant knew what could substitute the need for a VC. 'We mixed debt very correctly and were lucky to make the least mistakes. We built a hygienic way of looking at our business. In retrospect, I feel blessed that we did not expand in a hundred properties, which we would have if we had an investor. Instead, we chose to be super conservative.'

When I asked him how he managed without an investor for three years, he said,

> We ran a different model altogether. We completely shifted to an asset-light model. We had zero investment in real estate and capital during these four years and still grew at 20 per cent CAGR [compound annual growth rate]. We found ways to have partnerships with suppliers, distributors, factories and points of sale, and shared profitability with them. Instead of getting money from investors, we made the suppliers our investors, involving them. We had hundreds of investors that way. We started sharing our profits and had a three-sixty degrees partnership. We tweaked everything, and we got debt instead of equity. Whatever we learned from that period, we continue to do that even after getting an investor. We now have debt, equity and investment of our suppliers.

The smartest move, according to him, was that from 2012 onwards the company got rid of all non-profitable projects, all non-performing assets, which it would have not done had there been an investor. 'We closed one hundred and twenty points of sale. Still, our revenue remained the same. We made all possible corrections; we ensured every penny we made in business made sense.'

There are numerous cases where entrepreneurs take quick decisions that require heavy investment but later realise that it could have been done wisely. For instance, Kunal Bahl, the founder of the heavily VC-backed e-commerce firm Snapdeal, wrote an email to his employees in February 2017 when the company sacked around six hundred employees:

> Over the last two-three years, with all the capital coming into this market, our entire industry, including ourselves, started making mistakes. We started growing our business much before the right economic model and market fit were figured out. We also started diversifying and starting new projects while we still hadn't perfected the first or made it profitable. We started building our team and capabilities for a much larger size of business than what was required with the present scale. Ambition is critical because that's what motivates us to give our very best every single day – to achieve the undoable. However, a large amount of capital with ambition can be a potent mix that drives a company to defocus from its core. We feel that happened to us.[11]

The Business of VCs and PEs: How Do They Work?

VCs look for extremely high growth and exceptional profits from the companies they invest in, which entrepreneurs sometimes fail to understand. Limited partnerships (LPs) from whom VCs and PEs raise money have even higher expectations. Deep Kalra, who founded MakeMyTrip in 2000, recalls his early days of entrepreneurship, when, in 2001, a VC firm eVentures committed $2 million to his company before pulling out suddenly. Remember the dot-com bust of 2000? The dot-com boom, between 1995 and 2000, saw enormous money being invested in internet businesses across the world. And when the bust came in 2000, money worth $5 trillion was wiped out of the global economy. Only the best internet businesses such as eBay and Amazon survived. The bust also impacted internet companies in India. In 2001, when eVentures committed money into MakeMyTrip, Softbank and News Corp, the LPs of eVentures, decided not to invest in internet companies worldwide as a consequence of the dot-com bust. This is how the VC business works.

'So now I understand how it works,' said Kalra. 'One fine day, the LPs say they want your [VC] money back.' Start-ups can scale up only to a point the LPs believe in the idea at a macro level. The unfortunate part of a scenario like the dot-com bust when investors' money goes down the drain is not just the loss of money in terms of wealth but also the time, skills and effort of people, which go into building the companies. What happened with Kalra and his company signifies how global markets affect Indian companies. While global downturns affect the Indian economy, it is not necessary that a global boom in a specific sector will result in a parallel boom in the Indian market. The Indian market is very different from global markets, especially in the start-up space, which is precisely the reason why Ola and Snapdeal were different from their US counterparts Uber and Amazon in the early days.

Hence, if a global investor expects a company to grow at a certain rate, one must think of how India works. The Indian economy is different, and so are the consumers. Most entrepreneurs take their lessons from global examples, which can be problematic. This was, however, not the case with Sanjeev Bikhchandani, the founder of Info Edge, one of the few profitable internet companies in India. When he launched Naukri.com, an online job portal, in 1997, he had already been an entrepreneur for seven years. Nobody in the country knew what VC was, and Bikhchandani did not know of anybody who had taken VC money. 'Our concept was that we had to break even somehow and were growing from internal accruals. There were only fourteen thousand internet accounts in the country at that time [April 1997]. You could say that Naukri.com was a nifty idea,' Bikhchandani told me. He had no idea about the dot-com bubble and the big numbers people threw around about valuations of internet companies. Around mid-1999, Naukri.com began getting phone calls from investors, and Bikhchandani was baffled by the interest investors had in India at that time: 'For the life of me, I had been an entrepreneur – yes – but nobody had ever called to give me money. In 1992, I had to struggle for six months to get an overdraft limit of ₹30,000 from the State Bank of India. I still went for the meeting where an investor had called me.'

Bikhchandani did what many entrepreneurs miss doing today: to contemplate whether they need the money and if it is the right time for them to raise money. More importantly, he realised the differences between the expectations of global investors and the reality of India:

> I met a mid-twenty–something NRI who wanted to invest in Naukri.com. He wanted to put $2 million [around ₹8 crore] into our company. A dollar was then ₹40, and I quickly started doing the math in my mind. I could not comprehend that number. Naukri.com was ₹36 lakh in revenue then, that is, ₹3 lakh a month. I asked him [the potential investor] what will we do with so much money? He said, we will invest in the brand,

barrier to entry, and then after six months, we will raise another round, and one year from now, we will list you on Nasdaq.

The chat between the investor and Bikhchandani shows a typical case of over-expectations from a young start-up.

He laughed as he told me, 'I thought this guy is smoking dope. *Hamare yahaan voltage hai 160; AC kaam nahin karte.* There is no way we can list anywhere but on Paharganj, forget Nasdaq.' Bikhchandani did not want to do anything foolish. Though he was tempted by ₹8 crore funding he could have got then, he walked away. 'I said to myself that running a small company out of a house was not a bad thing. I thought I have done ₹36 lakh revenue this year; I will do another ₹50 lakh next year, and I will be happy. I did not want to build a big company,' he said. A few years later, when competition crept in, Info Edge raised ₹7 crore from an Indian investor and got listed on the National Stock Exchange of India (NSE). Diversified into four business portfolios, Info Edge is most popularly known for its recruitment division Naukri.com, which makes 75 per cent of its total revenue.[12] Its other verticals include matrimony (Jeevansathi.com), real estate (99acres.com) and education (Shiksha.com).

The most profitable consumer internet companies in India were built when VCs were not 'sexy' yet. VCs came late in their life. Investors bet on these start-ups when they knew the cars (read companies) were already running and that they just needed some fuel to run faster. Most internet companies globally, including Facebook (for popular or unpopular reasons), have a proven business model. If some of the Indian companies are to replicate that model, they should be able to have a vision of when they will be profitable.

Businesses should not shut down without external funding. If they do, they are doing something wrong. Many times, entrepreneurs are imperceptive of other sources of funding except VC investors. Padmaja Ruparel, the founding partner of Indian Angel Network (IAN), who meets an average of three hundred early-stage entrepreneurs every year, told me,

> Entrepreneurs must understand what kind of money they need. Venture capital is a twenty-five to thirty years phenomenon. I am not talking about the boom of VCs that came much later after 2007, which is when they started creeping in. So, one can safely say that the best businesses in India till now have been built without VC money. They were built based on two or three principles. One of the best ways to do business is through customer revenue. That has fed and is feeding so many businesses even today. Second, debt has always existed. Debt is not difficult for lateral-based businesses. Getting money is one of the inputs for building a business not the only input. Start-ups must introspect on the kind of money they need.

Padmaja while speaking to one such entrepreneur asked him why he needed millions in funding. She said, 'Why aren't you using debt? Why aren't you using the simple, old, traditional mechanism of raising money? Why are you diluting yourself for $2 million?' He could have easily raised half that amount in debt. According to her, the cheapest form of raising money is through grants, and then comes customer revenue, debt, equity and VC money, in that order.

MakeMyTrip's Kalra also believes that VC money is not the only way to drive a business. After the funding pullback by eVentures in 2001, Kalra managed to raise capital in 2005 from Sequoia Capital India (now called Peak XV Partners), but he had learned something by then:

> I think when you really have conviction in your business, you will do it even without funding. So at that time [in 2001], it came down to whatever money we had of our own. The only way was to borrow from friends and family. The difference

> between having a VC and friends/family as investors is that with the latter you know you need to return their money to them. When you get an investor, you share the pain and gain when the business goes bust or boom. With friends and family, you cannot hide from them – you have to return.

However, companies must raise money when they have to. The critical question to ask is when is the right time to do so, and even more critical is to say no to funds when you don't need them desperately for the decent growth of your company. After building the MakeMyTrip brand in the US, Kalra decided in 2005 to start operations in India, which was a five times costlier affair. Nobody understood internet marketing then. All the campaigning had to either be done on TV or hoardings. That was the only way to get people on the internet. When a funding opportunity came again, Kalra did an about-turn. 'I was clear we will need at least $20 to $30 million to build a brand in India, and then we did raise $10 million from SAIF Partners in 2005. I was just being pragmatic. I had to eat my own words back in 2005. After eVentures, I had thought I will never take money from a VC.'

Question Yourself: Why Venture Capital?

The temptation to raise money is often so high that one forgets to ask themselves the most obvious questions. Paras Chopra of Wingify conveyed this sentiment aptly when he said,

> Whenever you talk to a VC and the next question they ask is how you will spend this money, if you do not have a clear answer in mind, think again. If you are not able to answer this question clearly, it all comes down to whether are you doing this [raising funds] to get a media article in TechCrunch. If yes, it is a very expensive way of doing it.

Paras always had cash in the bank to run the business, so additional money would not have changed anything dramatically apart from the pace at which the top line of his company may grow. When a company's growth is not limited by capital but by other factors such as leadership quality, innovation and focus on customers, it is on the right track. With a lot of early-stage companies, growth is never limited to the amount of capital they have. 'In fact, VC money becomes a distraction,' Paras said. 'For some entrepreneurs, controlling where to take the company is way too important. Investor committees taking decisions on how the company should function is the last thing you want as an entrepreneur. Control, for me, is way more important than funding.'

Wait till You Are Ready to Raise Capital from a VC

Self-funded businesses tend to ask themselves consistently whether they should be raising capital or not. In 2010, Sunil Patro's company SignEasy was incubated by Microsoft Accelerator, which did not give any capital to Patro and hence there was no equity exchange as well, a major reason for him to be a part of the accelerator programme. SignEasy is a cloud-based e-signature solution for smartphones, tablets and computers. When I interviewed him in the early days of his business, he said,

> Every quarter, we think of raising capital. We feel everybody is raising capital, and we too are compelled to talk to investors. We did so for some time. But what we felt about the start-up ecosystem in India was different. We spoke to a few investors, and I realised that it was not my cup of tea. First, trying hard to raise money, and then, second, thinking of spending that money over the next two to five years. That is the time frame

> they [investors] need a plan for. I felt that building a product and growing the company through acquiring more customers is more joyful than getting an investor and raising capital. Knowing that you have to grow 10x in x number of years and 20x in another x number of years is not that exciting. I realised that I enjoyed the flexibility of my growth.

The trend in the start-up ecosystem to have VCs on board early on has been adopted from Silicon Valley. The statistic that we often miss is that India's economy is growing at 6 to 8 per cent, and if one cuts their living expenses as a start-up, it is not difficult to bootstrap and survive. On the contrary, in the US, the treadmill moves faster, and you can't survive without the support of VCs. Weighing in on the issue, Patro said,

> The reason why people raise money in the US is that it is more of a necessity. The cost of living is high, and unless you have exited a company in the past, you can't fund or bootstrap yourself. In the beginning, you cannot monetise. In the valley, you pretty much know you want to build a billion-dollar company, so you do what your surroundings tell you.

By December 2020, SignEasy had raised capital.[13] It received a round that included backers such as Girish Mathrubootham, CEO of FreshWorks. In a press statement following the funding, Patro said,

> It's time for us to tap into the expertise of entrepreneurs whose companies have scaled through serving the rapidly changing needs of small- and medium-sized businesses. Bootstrapping for as long as we did was by design; it wasn't until we had a sustainably profitable business – five years of consistently increasing revenue – that we felt comfortable having others' money at stake.

The fundamental question entrepreneurs should ask themselves is why are they building a business. Is it something that they love doing? Is it a problem – big or small – they want to solve? Are they doing it because there is a real need in the market? Or are they doing it because they want to chase money? Padmaja Ruparel of IAN put this in perspective: 'If chasing money is the reason, I am afraid it will be all the more difficult to get it. Investors will realise that this person is here to raise money only.' She said that in companies where people had their heads down and were busy building businesses, IAN went up to them and offered them money.

Now and Then

While entrepreneurs of the late nineties were different, so were investors at that time. Kalra speaks with the experience of being an investor and entrepreneur rolled into one:

> Today, when investors invest in companies, they are not necessarily looking at profits. In those days in 2005, I do not think investors had the appetite or gumption of taking too much loss. I think that has changed a lot. We were running a tight ship in a small office in Adchini [New Delhi] and we were breakeven as a business. We had given this much confidence to the investors *ki dhanda aata hai; paise banane aate hai.* I think both our investors got a lot of comfort from the fact that we managed on our own – that we had no funding.

According to him, people must bootstrap their businesses for as long as possible before saying, yes, now I am ready to take money. 'When I look back, that's how our investors looked at our story. They thought we could manage on our own, and a little bit of capital was worth investing in us.'

When I spoke with Kalra in 2016, it had been over eighteen years since he started MakeMyTrip. He continued to live his definition of success and confessed that he cannot imagine a day without MakeMyTrip in his life. He cannot envision it even on a long horizon. Kalra is now the chief mentor and group chairman of the company.

Today, it is fashionable for most businesses to raise VC money. To an extent, the media is responsible for the trend. In my initial days as a journalist, I was not interested in writing about companies that were not VC funded, perhaps because my fellow journalists never wrote about them. Journalists are often made to believe that only companies that are funded have a unique business model and are scaleable. For instance, in the year I started reporting (2009), only big-ticket capital investments made the news. By 2011, the media started covering smaller deals and start-ups became a beat. Still, even today, the obsession with funded companies remains, and few journalists talk about start-ups that are able to scale up without external capital. Even the ones that have been able to survive profitably in the competitive start-up world are not given the spotlight they deserve. Such businesses must be talked about and written about more frequently as a mission.

Karthik Sridharan, founder of Flexiple, however, has a slightly different approach. According to him, bootstrapped start-up founders need to tell their own stories rather than depend on the media:

> Media outlets don't pick up bootstrapped start-up stories very easily, and possibly not at all. I think, to a certain extent, the fact that bootstrapped start-ups don't have deep pockets and aren't supported by big organisations and institutions could work in their favour in terms of perception. I think people want to root for them deep down. Such start-ups just need to give these

people a reason and share their personal stories. Bootstrapped start-ups need to share their unique perspective on why they're building what they're building.

How do self-funded businesses make it? What choices do they make to attract more customers? From pricing to global aspirations and the challenge to retain employees, what are the strategies adopted by successful, funded businesses? This book provides all the choices and techniques essential for a successful business. You can pick the ones that suit yours.

2

Acquiring Customers in a Data-Driven Age in India

Two young employees of an HR tech start-up meet me every Thursday at 4 pm at the coworking place I operate from in Berlin. Liam Hao was a product designer from Hong Kong and Anna Boguslavska was a young product marketing manager from Kyiv, Ukraine. They were working in a stealth start-up and would visit the coworking space weekly to test their product. They took notes voraciously every time I gave them feedback about their product. I loved receiving their start-up newsletters and was genuinely interested in what they were creating. In fact, I might have been one of their early subscribers. Oh, wait! I forgot to mention that I've interviewed the founder of this young start-up. His passion was palpable. As we talked, his words transmogrified into products – not because of my imagination but because of his energy and clarity of thought. I don't know whether the start-up still exists or not. It might have died already or may have become a product with millions of subscribers. One thing is for sure though. The fate of any start-up depends on the product it creates, and feedback from the first few users are critical just like the first few readers of this book will decide whether it is worth recommending or not.

Early adopters of a product or a service are typically its founder's friends, family and well-wishers. Even if the first customer is not a friend or a family or a well-wisher, they are likely to be the most loyal customers in the long run if a personal connection is established through the team. (In my case, the two young employees who took my feedback seriously will play in my mind if I were to consider unsubscribing to the product or buying a paid version.) Whenever I have interviewed early customers, including corporates, or users of any product, the stickiness of the product is never its features but the team's eagerness to tweak the product as per the users' needs. Customers often have strong connections or a sense of familiarity with the team that is building the product. It is however not easy to tweak a product when it has reached a certain scale where the product offering has been standardised, catering to different customer segments. This, of course, is with reference to the pre-launch or early stage of a product.

Should You Trust All Data Blindly?

Getting customers for your business is not a choice but a necessity, and before we get on the customer acquisition journeys of different start-ups, it's important to state the role of data in the process.

We're talking about a time when defining a customer was not easy. We did not have data-driven marketing personas then. All that these founders knew was that they had to make money, and there was no other option to survive. A part of me still believes that every person in an Indian household is different, and the toughest market does define consumer personas.

Moreover, data is not always reliable when it comes to understanding why people chose a product. In a *Harvard Business Review* article published in 2020, authors Catherine Tucker and Nico Neumann even questioned the authenticity of data of consumers collected by the 'data brokers', who sell this data gathered from loyalty cards, public records, social media posts, etc., most often by tracking their browsing behaviour across different websites.[1] Collecting and selling data about people is estimated to be a $200 billion business, and all signs point to the continued growth of the data brokerage business. But there's a problem. According to Tucker and Neumann, the process by which data brokers create these segments is kept secret for competitive reasons. This, unfortunately, means that marketing managers do not know whether they can trust the audience data being purchased despite the fact that this expenditure typically makes up a large portion of their media budgets.

I believe that some of the traditional hacks can help start-up founders in this data-driven age where companies mostly rely on Google Analytics to find their next deal. 'Growth' is now an over-abused word in the VC-backed start-up world. I have had long interactions with founders, and often, while they feel they have achieved growth numbers through various hacks and A/B testing, they really don't know the pulse of their customers. They even feel that they could never focus on the overall goal of the company because they need short-term growth to be presented in the next investor meeting. There's a tendency to identify a channel for growth and to keep investing in it until a number to please the investor has been achieved. Important and sensitive issues such as diversity and inclusion are often ignored in the race for growth. These are the foundational premise for long-term growth. If a social media advertisement performs better with blonde models and white men, why bother having people of colour?

In my interactions with start-up growth heads, I have often encountered this dilemma. One of the VC-backed growth-stage start-ups I consulted briefly had huge challenges integrating diversity and inclusion values in their marketing activities as social media advertisements with black women or people of colour did not give them the results they needed in terms of short-term growth in audience traffic and conversions. After three hours of conversations with the senior management of the start-up, it was clear that while they did sincerely want to create an inclusive brand, they were aware of the possible face-off with their investors if they did not achieve the projected numbers. This is the kind of situation where the brand and the marketing performance team have views that are poles apart and the founder often becomes the peacemaker, eventually succumbing to short-term growth numbers.

The Promise of Product–Market Fit

So, how did these start-ups function when they did not have the money, knowledge or resources to make sales or when they knew nothing about their potential customers? In the early 2000s, Rajul Garg, founder of GlobalLogic, a digital product engineering company, and his co-founding team of engineers knew the technology they were building but lacked customer acquisition skills. On a global platform, many of us may not associate Garg's name with GlobalLogic as he exited the firm before it became famous. Post his exit, the firm got heavy funding and was later acquired by another firm. Now, GlobalLogic is headquartered in San Jose, California. The company has a revenue of over $550 million.[2] Today, Garg's name is conspicuously absent on the GlobalLogic website, which makes me question his definition of success in this story.

Garg and his team initially struggled to acquire customers until Peter Harrison joined as the CEO. Harrison's entry completely changed the game. GlobalLogic was founded in 2000 with a delivery centre in Noida, India. Much later, they got investors and new acquirers. All this would not have happened if the company was unable to acquire customers in the early days. Sharing his experience on LinkedIn, Peter Harrison said,

> [I] Joined GlobalLogic as a founding CEO when it was just two dozen employees and led its growth to over 6,000 [employees] with design studios and innovation hubs on four continents; raised financing from Sequoia Capital, Goldman Sachs, NEA and Draper Atlantic; led the company for over a decade to the point where it worked with 80 per cent of the top global technology brands to design and build innovative products through its global innovation hubs and design studios across the US, Argentina, Germany, India, Israel, Ukraine and the United Kingdom [between 2001 and 2013].[3]

Garg, though, has his own explanation. 'We were running out of money. We had no sales, and at the same time, the 9/11 attack happened in the US. It was complete pandemonium, basically. We had two to three months of money left, and then the planes hit, so whatever remaining hope there was, was basically completely gone,' he said of the dark phases of GlobalLogic.

This must be a familiar space for many. Almost every start-up goes through this phase of having to decide whether to shut down due to lack of funds or to stretch it and bleed. It gets all the more difficult if you are a group of tech enthusiasts without a sales budget. If no one buys your product or service, you add more tech features to it. Without Harrison and his sales knowledge, the company would have been dead, as per Garg. Building a product is not enough; it must be saleable too. You need to build, tell and sell.

Build and Tell

By focusing only on building in isolation and not taking customer feedback regularly, many founders, including some like Paras Chopra, have burnt their fingers. However, Paras now is heavily involved in all marketing activities through his personal brand, Twitter handle and rich content on his blogs. On the tenth anniversary of Wingify, Paras wrote on Twitter,

> Having attempted several start-ups during my undergraduate days and seeing all of them flop, I had come to realise the value of marketing and started learning about it. However, the more I read about marketing, the more I fell in love with it. After a while, it dawned on me that perhaps my next start-up should be about marketing. And that is how Wingify was born.[4]

It is true that users necessarily do not care about how passionate the founder of a product is. They don't care about how attached the founder is to the product and definitely don't have the time to understand the product. Their only motivation is the ease of usage – one click, one line, one message. But if you don't love your product, you will never be able to sell it.

This is what separates founders who live and breathe their products and services from the rest. Founders such as Paras Chopra (Wingify), Nithin Kamath (Zerodha) and Sridhar Vembu (Zoho) deeply love what they have built. They can talk about their products endlessly on various communication channels. They are not insecure about sharing everything they have learned on their way because they know that they hold sole proprietorships of this deep attachment to the product. They are not scared that someone will copy their processes. In fact, they want to share most things as they know that their vision is long-term and not as easy to replicate for someone looking for short-term gains.

Often the argument goes around 'product–market fit' or 'market-fit product', but Naval Ravikanth, an Indian-American entrepreneur and investor, and the co-founder, chairman and former CEO of AngelList, advocates for 'founder–product–market fit,[5] where founders are so passionate about what they do that they live their truest dreams, a sentiment I saw in most founders interviewed for this book. Ravikanth elaborates this on his podcast: 'Often, the best companies are ones where the product is an extension of the founder's personality, which shouldn't be a big surprise since everyone is passionate about themselves.'

Sales channels have drastically changed in the last ten years, evolving every six months. Today, your start-up might survive even without a Peter Harrison. Starting up, building a product and putting it up on Google Play Store or Apple App Store are not as difficult these days. The entry barriers are lower than what they were ten years ago. But the catch is to have something that people want to pay for.

Arpit Mehta, who has been a part of the leadership team at the Indian start-up ClearTax, spoke about the importance of marketing in the context of one of his earlier start-ups. 'One must figure out marketing/sales before building a product – even sell it before actually building it. Someone paying for the idea or concept is the best validation,' he said. 'In my previous start-up, an e-learning company, we did our first sales pitch on a mere PowerPoint presentation. Then we developed high-end animations and simulations once we validated the product through the needs of the customer.' It is always useful to go and pitch your idea to customers and keep adding features to your product.

Another important aspect is to start small and gradually build up. Sridharan of Flexiple rightly said that there's a lot of popular narrative in start-up media and tech media that you need to build something scaleable. 'There are just so many buzzwords around the kind of technologies that are used; you'll hear AI [artificial intelligence] or ML [machine learning] one year and then NLP [natural language processing] the next year, and after that comes blockchain and the current media darlings Web3 and the metaverse,' he said. 'Every entrepreneur feels that unless they're using any one of these technologies, they aren't even building something for scale. Are they going down the right path?'

Sridharan also made the same mistake: instead of focusing on how they should get their first ten users (they had zero people using their product at the time), they wanted a million users immediately. They thought about all the problems that might occur if a million users started using their product. The problem with that thought process is that you don't know what your users will do or what problems you'll face until you've had some experience. 'Unless you get to a certain position in the market and understand what the market is, there's only so much that user research and surveys can tell you. I think you actually need to do business – to make your users pay money – to understand what they truly feel about interacting with you,' he said.

According to Sridharan, there are two types of start-ups. The first type is core tech start-ups, where the technology being developed is the main product that people buy. The second type is tech-enabled start-ups, where the product or service is not solely based on technology. Technology is used to help grow the business. To start, focus on finding a solution to the problem you're solving for your customers. Make sure the solution is simple and effective even if it requires manual work. It's important that the solution is a perfect fit for your customers. Only after you have a solid solution, you can think about using technology to scale it. Once you have the solution figured out, you will uncover any obstacles and better understand your customers' needs.

Do Channel Partners Make Sense for All Business Models?

There are numerous ways through which you could start selling your products. The most common one is through strategic partnerships and existing networks most commonly known as network effects. Remember how most of us started using Paytm in 2014? It was known as a digital wallet at that time. Later, Paytm started offering its customers a range of funding sources: Paytm UPI, Paytm Wallet, Paytm Payments Bank account, debit card, credit card and netbanking.[6]

Another smart move by Paytm was a tie-up with taxi service company Uber in India, which made so many of us become early adopters of the app/product. Automatic Paytm accounts were created for Uber users. Identifying strategic partners and then leveraging their user base is a good idea. If Paytm had not existed, Uber would have had to find an innovative way to create a user base in India. In 2014, Indian consumers were still cash-dependent, with cash on delivery as the preferred mode of payment on e-commerce and Uber's rival Ola accepting payment only in cash. When Uber entered India, One97 Communications–owned Paytm became the sole payment channel for Uber. While the details of the revenue-sharing agreement between the parties were not shared with the media, it is understood that Paytm received about 2.5 per cent of every transaction recorded on Uber.

Allen Penn, the then head of the Asia market at Uber, had expressed confidence in the strategic mindset behind the partnership: 'With the Paytm tie-up, more than 600 million people who have bank accounts and netbanking will be able to enjoy the seamless and cashless experience that credit card users experience with Uber. It's a fully in-app wallet customised experience, which is a great example of the importance of the Indian market.'[7]

What this and the 2016 demonetisation did for Paytm could be considered two of the most important customer acquisition waves for the company. On 8 November 2016, when the Government of India announced the demonetisation of all ₹500 and ₹1,000 banknotes of the Mahatma Gandhi series, it also announced the issuance of new ₹500 and ₹2,000 banknotes to replace the demonetised banknotes. Overnight, all cash of the said denominations became worthless paper as the government stopped recognising them as legal tender. This led to households struggling to pay for groceries and other daily expenses. In such a dire situation, Paytm Wallet was a real godsend, and people flocked to it in droves. It went from one hundred twenty-five million wallet customers before demonetisation to one hundred eighty-five million in just three months, and it continued to grow, hitting three hundred twenty-five million wallet users by 2021.[8]

These are the things that blow my mind about India as a country. Nowhere else in the world could sudden sociopolitical conditions create a situation in which the revenue of a start-up such as Paytm changes favourably overnight. While this was a blockbuster move by Paytm, it also gave a tough time to many other start-ups at the same time.

When I spoke with a Hyderabad-based entrepreneur Ashok Reddy the morning after demonetisation, he was a hassled man. It had much to do with what happened the day before. Reddy's phone did not stop ringing the morning after the demonetisation announcement; he was busy wondering how he would manage the same number of orders in his business for the next two to three months. At the time, he was running a start-up called MyWholesaler, a web-based B2B platform in the grocery space, which catered to the needs of retailers who experience gaps in the existing arrangements and are looking at facilities beyond just stock procurement. Reddy sold products to retailers in a more organised way than other distributors. On average, he used to get around one hundred twenty orders a day, but after the demonetisation, more than half of them cancelled or postponed because local retailers were facing a cash crunch. Reddy's delivery van drivers were now more than willing to exchange their demonetised ₹1,000 notes for ₹10 bundles, which they would often refuse. Reddy's challenge was only the tip of the iceberg. Small and medium enterprises (SMEs) and entrepreneurs operating in rural areas were under tremendous stress.

Despite all the challenges, start-ups felt that there was a bright light at the end of the tunnel. They told me that they only needed to find innovative ways to sustain themselves for the next two to six months. Reddy too knew what would work for him:

> I just need to increase my customer base from two thousand retailers right now to five thousand. I can envision the benefits of this effort by the government in the long run. A company like mine will have more acceptance by retailers; they will have no reason to pay me just in cash. The next three to four months will be tough, but eventually, retailers will have to use mobile wallets and deal in a more structured way through our mobile app.

Three years later (2019), even though demonetisation had had some adverse effects on different parts of the economy, one of the few sectors that benefitted from this step was digitisation. The government pushed for a less-cash society by increasing infrastructure to allow digital payments. In most tier-II and tier-III towns, digital payments doubled in the three years since demonetisation. From global technology giants such as Google and Amazon to a few of the country's biggest mobile wallets including Paytm and MobiKwik, all adopted the digital payments system.

Digital payments in India work on the back of UPI, or Unified Payments Interface. UPI is a platform that merges various banking services and features under one umbrella. A UPI ID and PIN are sufficient to send and receive money. Real-time bank-to-bank payments can be made using a mobile number or virtual payment address (UPI ID). It doesn't matter if it's a smartphone or a basic feature phone. UPI is an initiative undertaken by the National Payments Corporation of India (NPCI) together with India's central bank, the Reserve Bank of India (RBI), and the Indian Banks Association (IBA). NPCI is the firm that handles RuPay payments infrastructure, similar to Visa and MasterCard. It allows different banks to interconnect and transfer funds.

As of 2021, UPI managed to oversee thirty-eight billion transactions worth ₹71.59 trillion with over two hundred fifty banks on its roster.[9] It's one mainstream digital financial technology that is unique to India, keeping India's shoulders above even developed countries.

Your Customers Don't Know You Exist, Especially in India

Getting more women on a dating app is a struggle even for a global start-up, but imagine if you were one of the first dating apps in India back in 2015. It would be even harder because of cultural backgrounds. I am an independent, educated woman from a middle-class Delhi family, yet I did not have the guts to let ten men in a radius of 5 km know that I was single and looking for love or a date. Times have changed now, but dating apps have had their own share of struggles in the transition.

One of the early players in the dating app market was TrulyMadly founded by Sachin Bhatia, who had earlier had a stint with MakeMyTrip before starting his own company. TrulyMadly managed to raise money but didn't want to splurge on marketing, so it entered into partnerships with non-competing brands to promote itself. Bhatia learned a few lessons from his job at MakeMyTrip, which he applied at his new company, TrulyMadly. They wanted more women on the app, but where would they find these potential customers? Maybe on an online lingerie store where women are not only active in the digital world but also, in Bhatia's words, more progressive and confident. 'We did a campaign with Zivame, an online lingerie brand, where it was about the right fit. It was about both a bra fitting a girl well and [the girl] finding the right match on a dating app,' he said. Shying away from mass media, TrulyMadly focuses on the digital medium to establish its brand identity, reach out to their primary target audience of millennial women and stand out with brand communication. The rationale behind this was simple: all its potential customers were online and spent a significant amount of time on their mobiles. Not falling into the trap of simply leveraging mass media for marketing, Bhatia figured out a way to reach out to its potential audience in a way that did not break the bank. All their marketing campaigns were directed at women because they were the core audience. The idea behind targeting them was that once they came on the app, men and other genders interested in women will follow.

The rationale behind the brand's quirky campaigns was that they would resonate with the target group, make it stand apart in the dating app category, remove taboos about dating and lighten the air around it. Bhatia said in a media interview,

> In the West, the audience easily transmitted to the apps from the web medium. But in India, there was hardly any online dating prevalent before the apps. Hence, we wanted to roll out a campaign that drove home the message to the girls that there is no harm in window shopping. Just look at the boys that are available and browse their information. It is a new concept for the audience as well, so in case they liked what they saw, they would come back to the app.[10]

Since all of TrulyMadly's communication was targeted towards women, association with women-only brands was but a natural progression of their digital marketing strategy.

FIG 2.1 A 2015 media campaign of the dating app TrulyMadly[11]

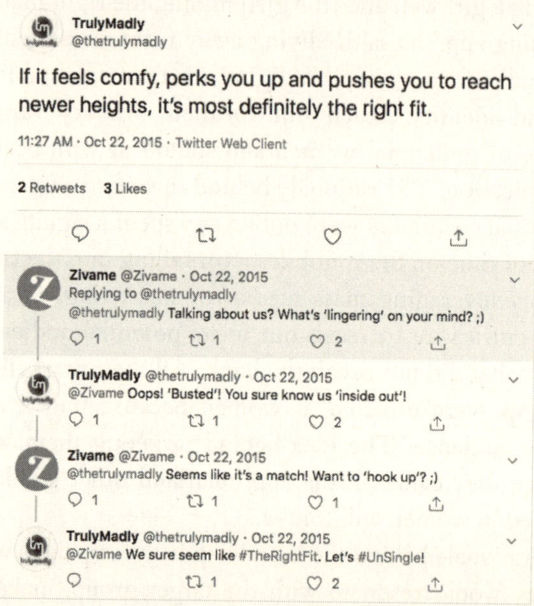

No Budget for a Sales Team

One of the most interesting stories about acquiring customers and channel partners was that of RateGain's, a Noida-based company that provides SaaS solutions to hotels, OTAs, airlines, tour operators and car rental companies, empowering them with data and business intelligence. Bhanu Chopra, the founder of the company, did not have the budget to hire a sales team to sell to hotels so they found a technology company that was already selling to hotels and partnered with them. 'We decided to collaborate with the partners who were already selling to our customers. We gave them an incentive of a large revenue share. We said we would pay them 89 per cent of the share, but they have to get us "x" number of customers in two years,' Bhanu told me. RateGain gave them an exclusive sales partnership. Bhanu first identified a partner who had all its customers and sweetened the deal as much as he could. He said,

> They took care of all the customer support, customer engagement, and we just had to provide the technology. In a SaaS environment, once you make a product, you can sell it to as many customers. The incremental variable cost is low. We wanted to sell to companies that have thousands of hotel customers. This meant we were dealing only with one channel partner, enabling us to scale. We became prudent and calculated backwards and realised how essential it is that we always have a buffer.

This strategy got RateGain instant scale and provided an opportunity to capture a large audience.

If you are wondering if it was a smart strategy for RateGain, the story gets interesting. It definitely worked at that time and got them customers, but something else happened after they signed them on as strategic partners.

The channel partner realised the potential in this business and acquired a competitor of RateGain in 2011. Bhanu though did not disclose the name of the channel partner and the competitor to me.

The year 2011 was terrible for RateGain as they had to restart after losing 80 per cent of their customers and revenue. This completely changed Bhanu's mindset about customer acquisition. He was circumspect when he said,

> Now, we do not follow the revenue-sharing model. We have a number of channel partners and offer them 20–25 per cent share and not insane amounts. The company was just a price comparison B2C site when we started. The market is extremely competitive, and we have to innovate constantly. So we started providing recommendations and analytics to hotels, and tell them how to price and help facilitate their knowledge about how much others are charging.

It's difficult to say for sure if the strategy was wrong. It probably was not implemented well. Some due diligence and contract norms could have saved RateGain from that mishap.

What Is a Minimum Viable Product? Is It Dead?

Zoho, a unicorn technology company that makes web-based business tools, is one of India's most successful bootstrapped stories. One would imagine that Sridhar Vembu, the CEO of this SaaS start-up, was clear on the idea of a minimum viable product, or MVP, for his company. But here is what he has to say about the obsession with MVPs: 'Our problem today is that we create these concepts without understanding how they can actually be implemented in real business situations. A minimum viable product is a good concept, but it doesn't have divine sanctity; it doesn't mean that you should always launch a minimum viable product. It depends on the markets.'

He gives an example: no one is going to buy a mobile phone that is a minimum viable product because there are so many sophisticated, really good mobile phones at really attractive prices. He adds,

> If I have to compete in that market, I have to put together a really good product that stands up against the competition. We create a start-up theology with the ten commandments. That's the wrong way to think about it. Many of them are useful thumb rules; you have to use your discretion to judge whether it is a wise decision. People are seeking formulas for success always, but the truth is that there is no such formula for success.

Sridharan of Flexiple, which by 2021 had a revenue of $3 million, went back to the idea of 'just doing it' and understanding your customers. The problem is that founders start building their products directly from a technology point of view, thinking that technology will be the absolute messiah that will solve all the different issues their customers might face. That's possibly not the most intelligent approach because you don't know all the problems you're going to face. He spoke of a similar mistake his team made:

> Spending $5,000 on this vision of tech or scale might not seem like a significant amount, but when you're bootstrapping, it was all our savings. We soon realised that we were going about it all backwards. We just needed one freelancer for each talent requirement that a company comes to us since we were building a pool of freelancers for clients. So we just opened a

> Google Sheets with one tab called companies and another called freelancers. We started reaching out to companies through our network and then to freelancers over LinkedIn and updated our list. That Google Sheets was our MVP. Next, we manually emailed potential freelancers and clients to make the match.

Sridharan did this till Flexiple made $100,000 in revenue, but then maintaining the Google Sheets started getting tiresome. His company also began facing bottlenecks. The next question was how to automate the process using technology. 'By then, we were not solving fictitious problems; we were facing them. So we knew the exact situations to solve, which would take us to the next level of scale. So the basic idea that scale is absolute because it's a million users is false,' he said. 'I am not saying you shouldn't have a vision for your start-up, but your vision versus execution doesn't have to be the same. And that's where I think we faltered, and many start-ups falter even today.'

The Zoho Bootstrapping Strategy: Build, Build, Build!

Zoho's business was not in a direct consumer-like product market. They were operating in a highly specialised product market space. Hence, traditional marketing made the most sense to Vembu at that time. To expand on it, he said,

> There may have been only three hundred potential customers for the product all over the world when we started. So what do you do? You go to a trade show, a very industry-specific trade show, and you meet some potential customers and they express an interest in your software. Then you arrive at some kind of licensing model. So it was a highly customised model, and we did not think of product sales the way we're thinking about it

> today. But that isn't the only way to do it. I am just saying this is one way to think about things. If you develop a specialised technology in some niche, somebody might be interested in it, and that somebody might be willing to pay for it. You take that money as your seed capital – that's what you think of as your seed capital.

But how does one deal with a competition that has more resources and cash to expand than you do? Zoho's biggest competitor has always been Salesforce. Vembu fearlessly wrote in his blog titled 'They Acquire, Acquire, Acquire While We Build, Build, Build' in 2013 about this competition:

> The Salesforce playbook is simple. Benioff (founder, chairman and CEO of Salesforce) feels restless, he sees stagnation, sees companies like Zoho continuing to innovate, he just goes out and does a blockbuster deal to feel good, more money the better. Who cares if the acquisition actually pays off long term? This playbook can only work as long as the stock price keeps levitating – and for that, let's give credit where it is due: it is not Benioff, it is Bernanke. How companies with continuing losses year after year could reach a valuation of nearly 10x annual revenue is a topic by itself, but that would take me on a major tangent on our broken bubble-blowing monetary policy, and the wanton stupidity of policy makers like Bernanke.
>
> I am putting my conviction to the test. We are expanding our investment in R&D in Zoho. We see a massive opportunity to seize leadership in the cloud because we believe the Salesforce strategy is going to fail long term. They already face engineering stagnation – their core SFA product hasn't improved in years. Second, they have to try to stick it to customers to make the money back on these blockbuster deals. The end result is that customers will revolt and seek alternatives. While our strategy of investing in R&D is slower in the short run, as we gain speed

> over time, our breadth and depth increases. Here is our promise to customers: we will continue to out-innovate Salesforce, while offering incredible value.
>
> How can we make that promise? Simply because we don't throw around money like them. We owe it to you, the customer, to be efficient, and pass on the results of efficiency in terms of lower prices. We don't do ego-boosting acquisitions to create hype in the short term, only to be forgotten a couple of years later. Instead, we hire engineers and write code because we believe that serves our customers better.
>
> Zoho is already beating Salesforce on internet reach, on the sheer number of new organisations signing up for our platform month after month. We will continue our relentless execution.[12]

Now, that was a brave blog post, written in 2013 but it got only a little over seventy-five hundred views as I write this book. I wonder if it was written and shared today, would it have caused a Twitter storm. This post was triggered by the Salesforce acquisition of ExactTarget, which competed with Zoho Campaigns products, and had about sixteen hundred employees, while all of Zoho Corp had about sixteen hundred employees by then.

I interviewed Zoho's top management twice for this book. When I spoke with Vembu, I had just started writing this book, and then I spoke to Raju Vegesna, the company's chief evangelist, when I was midway through the manuscript. Raju had mostly been operating from the United States since the inception of the company. His focus had been on making the product stellar. 'If you like a product, you'll recommend it to your friend, if you don't, you wouldn't. It's as simple as that, right? So, it comes down to just one thing: the product. Is it good enough?' he said. It felt like he was probing himself as he spoke. Probably that is what you constantly need to do with the product. Once you have a product that's excellent, you will provide a reason for people to talk about it, recommend it and adopt it for good.

In recent times, there has been a lot of discussion about whether the concept of MVP is still effective or not. Some people are leaning towards embracing the idea of a minimum awesome product (MAP) or a minimum lovable product (MLP) instead. These new terms suggest going beyond just a basic viable version of the product and aiming for something that is truly impressive and delightful.

The key difference between MVP, MAP and MLP lies in the level of customer experience and satisfaction they aim to achieve. While MVP focuses on creating a functional product with the minimum set of features, MAP and MLP emphasise creating a product that not only meets the basic requirements but also wows customers with its awesomeness or loveability.

However, it's important to note that the definition of MVP or whether it's still relevant will depend on the competition you face in the market. You need to ask yourself a crucial question: are you better than what already exists, so much so that people would be willing to switch to your product?

Ultimately, the goal is to create a product that not only solves a problem but also captivates users and surpasses their expectations. Whether you choose MVP, MAP or MLP, the key is to understand your customers' needs and preferences, and deliver a product that stands out and offers a superior experience compared to the alternatives.

The Thirty-Second Rule of Turning a Visitor into a Subscriber

After building a product, the second most important thing is discoverability, which means, are people able to discover you easily or find you through online search engines and other means? When they do find you, are you adding a barrier for them to try your products? Raju explained this with some clarity:

> In our case, we ask, 'Is a person able to try our products in less than thirty seconds or not?' If the answer is no, we've got to fix it. Sub thirty seconds, we want someone to sign up and just land in the product page right away. That improves the expression because they are coming in to buy your product, and so they should be able to try it. It should be extremely easy and that's certainly our goal.

By removing the friction, Zoho tried to make it easy for people to try the product. If they don't like it, they move on. And if that's not the right tool that they are looking for then maybe they move on to find another one.

If customers don't convert within thirty seconds of moving in, it is a bounce (they leave the website). My instant question to Raju was how to find out why people are leaving. How do you convert those?

> We don't worry too much about people who bounce. We basically worry about the people who are sticking with us and how to keep them happy. If we keep them happy, they will automatically bring in other people. Because they could be coming in, they would have landed here for a completely different reason, and there is no way to figure out why certain people are not converting. You can't survey millions of people. It's not practical.

Deep Kalra of MakeMyTrip also said something similar – that retaining customers is more important than acquiring new customers who come just for heavy discounts. However, when stuck in the growth game, most VC-run start-ups invariably focus on acquiring more and more customers who come in for heavy discounts.

As a start-up journalist, I had signed up for a lot of newsletters of young SaaS products, and I often replied to them. I'd write to find out how involved they were with customer engagement, but many times I didn't receive a reply.

Raju agreed with me that engaging with customers is a vital part of growing a business. He told me how they see and do things differently:

> Response is needed. But what a lot of companies do actively that we don't is that whenever someone signs up there is a lot of follow-up, say, about fifteen to twenty [emails], to convert them into a paying customer. In our case, we send maybe one or two follow-up emails at max and then leave it at that. We don't forcefully sell you something. That's actually a fairly simple thing: if somebody is really interested, they will sign up and try it and ask for it.

You don't need this book to tell you about the various customer acquisition channels. There are numerous articles to give you that knowledge. The more important thing to figure out is how to use these channels (and which ones) and how to train your team on customer relations. According to Wingify's Chopra, each and every person in the company knows how to make a good and genuine sales pitch. Every person in a start-up is a salesperson in their own way.

A lot of times founders excessively focus on online sales when the real gold mine is somewhere else. It is likely that this gold mine is not necessarily where the crowd is.

If you were to list all these channels, there are probably forty channels out there, from radio to TV advertisements to billboards, physical mailers, trade shows, online mailers, online promotions and marketplaces to whatnot. Then, of course, there's YouTube, Facebook and other social media channels too. These are all the biggest channels, and for a specific business, some of these channels make perfect sense, others don't. There's no generic advice here; all the channels have to be analysed on their own merits to be able to say, okay, I am going to focus on PR or offline media, and this may vary from country to country. For example, Raju said, Zoho does radio advertisements in India but not in the US. Why? Similarly, they do YouTube advertisements but not TV advertisements in Mexico. They do mailers in Canada but not in India. Depending on the market and product, each business should understand each of these channels; they have to figure out which one is apt for them based on the region.

Customer Feedback Is Fuel for Sales and Acquisition

Every product has a feedback button somewhere, mostly in the main column of the main profile section where they can click on a product and provide feedback. But the biggest feedback really comes from customer support. For Raju, this feedback loop is extensive and vigorous:

> We also have in-product support chat systems, and we are making it global across products where customers can directly chat with an online representative and ask for something or provide feedback. Then there are other ways of getting feedback, but for the most part, between support in product banners to chat, that covers, say, 70–80 per cent of the feedback. Of course, we get a lot of feedback at our events; we do about 100+ events worldwide – so trade shows and all of that. So from our own user events to our own community events, which are maybe a few hundred events worldwide, there are various feedback loops which are then internally posted for broader consumption.

Sell Abroad then Sell in India

Let me tell you a known secret: most successful and profitable companies in India started by selling abroad and then looked at India when they had the money to cash in on Indian customers. Zoho, MakeMyTrip, Directi, Wingify all took this route. Look at Zoho, for instance. What do you do when you find it difficult to sell in India or when you feel you have to pay to get additional customers? It's easy: you find your customers in markets that are ready to pay. Competing with Google and Microsoft shouldn't scare you. If I have to put it in candid words: most successful Indian products replicate global business models and sell abroad at cheaper prices. (More on me-too business ideas or business models in the next chapter.)

Why did all these start-ups have to first look at the US markets to make money? For Zoho, according to Raju, it's the conversion rate: 'In India, people like engaging with vendors a lot, but they don't buy as much. In India, customers expect pretty much everything for free. So the conversion rate, for example, is lower than the US's. I don't have the numbers in front of me, but I would say it's significantly lower.'

But engaged customers are good, aren't they? Well, this is a different kind of engagement for Raju:

> A lot of people get on the call, get a demo, all of that, and then they will say, you know, we'll use the free version, which is perfectly fine. Some of it is just the maturity of the market. This is totally expected when the market is just coming up. They're not comfortable putting up their credit cards online, and they're not used to paying for something on a subscription basis. The concept of 'credit card' itself in India is relatively new compared to, say, some of the Western countries. Which means conversion is going to be lower and that is expected.

While Zoho has always been present in India, according to Raju, it became a mature market for it after eighteen years of existence:

> When we started, the fundamental realisation was that India doesn't have the market for what we were doing, because we were selling to equipment manufacturers. How many equipment manufacturers did India have? Zero, precisely. How many routers and servers were created in India? Basically, zero. So India became the production centre for Zoho, while the target market was the US, Japan and Europe, where they were creating production equipment. But once we said, okay, India is going to evolve into a market, we started investing in it. And now India itself, certainly, given the current trends, is a market. And this was not a surprise. All along you can clearly tell when a market would be ready for a company to enter versus when it's not.

What Do International Markets Mean for Indian Companies Like Zoho? How Are We Competing with the Microsofts of the World?

Most markets internationally are corporate monoliths. They have one or two large companies that dominate the market with over 80 per cent market share. Silicon Valley thrives on the winner-take-all approach. But there's one good thing about the market system that people with a socialistic bias miss: markets have infinite segments. There's going to be, for whatever reason, a customer for whom the solutions offered may not meet their needs; one has to seek out and nurture that customer.

'In other words, you have to flip that question around. It's not like convincing someone in every case about why we are better than Salesforce and Microsoft,' Vembu of Zoho said. 'You find those market segments where you can shine and then you broaden the base. We are always competing with international brands. We already face Microsoft or Google in the US. So we'll face them in India; it's not like we aren't used to this.'

According to Vembu, the problem is that a lot of Indian brands focus only on India; they don't take the war abroad. This makes me believe that participating in international markets becomes much easier when you are a pure B2B start-up.

In defence of B2C start-ups, one can't even imagine Flipkart taking the retail fight to the US market without first acquiring Walmart, but companies such as Zoho would argue that is the only way to grow in the long term.

The primary market for Zoho in the beginning was the US and then Japan. In the late 1990s, Japan was the second-largest economy in the world. In 2017, Japan contributed to over 30 per cent of the company's revenues. Later, Zoho expanded to China. In the period when the US was reeling under the weight of the dot-com crash, China proved to be a good market.

However, Vembu is optimistic about India as a market and categorical about the politics and development of the nation:

> In the long term, I see India as a very strong market. A lot of demographics, skilled workforce, the spread of knowledge and there is a hunger for development in our country now. People want development. A lot of the politics itself is realigning that way. Politicians are competing on the track record of development, jobs, roads, electricity, etc. For example, in a lot of places now, power cuts are unacceptable. They used to be the norm in India. These are all new developments in the last ten to fifteen years. This is all the effect of a more market-oriented economy. India has shed its socialist past, now it's a freer country than, say, it was twenty to thirty years ago. Then the economy grows, GDP rises and technology intensity increases because you need technology to

> improve labour productivity. We are at the right time and the right place in India.

In 2019, close to 50 per cent of the company's business came from the US, about 30 per cent from Europe and 20 per cent from the rest of the world. The India market was growing so fast that Raju felt he wouldn't be surprised if India becomes their number two country moving forward, possibly in the next year or two years. Fast forward to 2022, India made almost 10 per cent revenue for Zoho, growing at the rate of 77 per cent year-on-year.[13]

Customer Acquisition in India

Selling consumer products in India can be a bigger hassle than running a B2B enterprise. Nearbuy is a hyper-local e-commerce company based out of India. I had a chat with Ankur Warikoo, its co-founder, when he was deeply involved in the operations of the company. He had a feet-on-street team that went and physically spoke to merchants on a daily basis. As a business, it allowed customers to discover and buy from merchants nearest to them. Nearbuy operated in all categories of 'stepping out' for the customer and functions like an online travel guide.

'This was always our model from the very beginning, and it is people intensive but not capital intensive unless you're equating people to capital,' said Warikoo, who has since moved on from Nearbuy and is now a well-known start-up and marketing influencer. 'There's an advantage to this. In terms of being very crowded, you can speak to all the restaurants in just one go and you capture all of them in just one go. That makes it easier from our efficiency perspective. About 92 per cent of all our merchants are still working with us.' said Warikoo.

Customers complained to Nearbuy on a regular basis but Warikoo was candid in saying that the complaints are directed at the places they bought from. Nearbuy is a marketplace for cheap deals in services. I once bought a Nearbuy restaurant discount coupon for a meal for two. When we arrived to avail it, the restaurant turned down the offer on account of the Indian festival Karva Chauth. Neither was this mentioned while buying the coupon nor anywhere on the restaurant website. No one was accountable for the service I bought. Nearbuy said they were just a marketplace and hence couldn't be held responsible, and the restaurant laid the blame squarely on me for buying directly from Nearbuy and not on their website. Customers look to Nearbuy for some assurance of a good experience even if it does not control the vendors' side of the business, and they will always hold it accountable. In some cases, it might be easy to acquire customers, but keeping them happy is an altogether different game.

Warikoo told me that Nearbuy had to work very closely with merchants to ensure that they understand what they are doing because at the end of the day, it's their customers: 'We win 93 per cent of the time but lose 7 per cent of the time. We go through a proper process. It's a three-step process, but after we go through that, we display reviews and ratings as is. That's where we are 100 per cent transparent.'

In 2017, Paytm announced the acquisition of Nearbuy. In a statement, Paytm said it arranged a merger of this well-funded start-up and made a 'strategic' investment in the resultant entity for a majority stake. The company statement said, 'Paytm's strategic holding in Nearbuy will provide Paytm's merchant partners an opportunity to offer deals to acquire new customers and grow their business. Additionally, Paytm will serve its large consumer base by showcasing a large number of exciting deals on its platforms.'[14] During this time, in 2019, Warikoo resigned from his position as CEO of Nearbuy.

In India, while access to potential customers may be easy, but acquiring and servicing them is tough. India is a price sensitive and competitive market where customers seek value over other things. It's also a large and diverse market, which makes it difficult to identify potential customers. Many times, companies are shooting in the dark. In Europe, under the General Data Protection Regulation (GDPR) guidelines, companies can't send out their newsletters randomly to customers unless they categorically sign up for them, forget calling customers and trying to sell products. One can imagine why entrepreneurs such as Nithin Kamath did what they did to acquire customers:

> In 2010, when I started, it was the worst time for brokerages ever for the world. My competitors weren't active because they were in a shell worrying, crying and being pessimistic, which gave us a big advantage. Today, the advantage we have is that we transformed from a brokerage firm to a fintech company. The first year, all the money I had was invested in this business. We lived month by month. The first year was such a rush that I was just making phone calls to potential customers to sell the product. It didn't feel like a business in the first year. There was no strategy.

The definition of fintech has changed drastically over the years in India, probably the fastest in the world. Nithin, who has seen it all, recalled the transformation. At the beginning, Nikhil, his brother, was trading and answering support calls. A few other guys and he were in the sales team. The team was small and agile, so decisions came fast. 'In the US, fintech is not about wallets, it's about money management as well,' he said. 'I think, looking back, what helped us grow was that no one interfered with us. Our decisions were taken swiftly.'

Zerodha started operations on 15 August 2010 with the goal of breaking all barriers that traders and investors face in India in terms of cost, support and technology. They named the company Zerodha, a combination of 'zero' and the Sanskrit word '*rodha*' (barrier). By 2020, their disruptive pricing models and in-house technology had made them the biggest stockbroker in India in terms of active retail clients. Today, in 2023, they have eight million users.

In 2017, Nithin was still excited when he told me about what they had achieved: 'We have moved from that to a trading platform where people actually buy. There are pieces which are still vendor-based. Adding clients to our business was a long, intense process because my clients had to sign a twenty-five-page booklet and give it to me. So initially there was a big resistance.'

By that time, Zerodha had become bigger than ICICI and Reliance in terms of exchange turnover. They got smaller yields because they charged flat fees. They were driven by tech, adding 13–14k clients every month at that time.

'Generally, business and finance are so complex that people's understanding is quite low,' Nithin said. 'So we made it really simple. We never had two offers on the table. That made running the operations simple.'

Customer acquisition channels might increase from one to hundred to thousand in a country such as India, but it is definitely one of the most challenging tasks to change the mindset of Indian customers.

In the 1990s, online selling was not even an option in India. Broadband connectivity was still at its nascent stage, so watching video advertisements on the internet was impossible. However, this was also the time when companies such as MakeMyTrip were born. Deep Kalra, MakeMyTrip founder, said,

> We focused on TV and did a commercial. We also did keyword searches and banners for online. So, one is getting people, then the product and technology and then retaining people on the product. These challenges are goals for different teams. Today, we had a three-hour session on customer loyalty. There are customers who come back to us twenty to thirty times and thousands who spend more than ₹10 lakh with us annually. We don't want to lose any one of them. I want long-term customers who do not get swayed by discounts and cashback.

These companies seem high on principle, but there are also companies with long-term visions, which is where high-growth start-ups may falter.

Raise money if you have to, but remember that you will not always acquire long-term customers. You may acquire customers who are users, who can show 'growth' in the next investor meeting, but if they are unhappy, they will leave you just as soon.

3

Do You Want Indians to Pay for Your Product?

Sumeetra was the cleaning lady who used to work in all the apartments in our building in India. When two of my friends and I moved into an apartment in the Greater Kailash area in New Delhi in 2017, we asked her if she would be willing to clean our apartment. She said she would do it for ₹1,500 per month. Our requirement, however, was only for that day, so we offered her ₹200 as a one-time fee. She denied our offer outright and said that either she would do it for a fixed monthly income or not at all. At that time, I thought she was taking advantage of us, but in retrospect, she was very clear about her pricing strategy. We ended up employing her for the entire month in desperation.

The same day, Pushkar (name changed), a close friend, came over for dinner. Unfortunately, he got bitten by a dog on his way back home. He went to a doctor the next day. The doctor gave him two options: post-exposure prophylaxis (PEP) anti-rabies vaccine or pre-exposure prophylaxis (PrEP) anti-rabies vaccine. There was a catch though. The second option was twice the price of the first. Pushkar saw value in the second option and took it. He took it because he was in pain and needed protection, that is, the pain made him appreciate the value of long-term protection against the virus.

Here is a quick tip. Indian customers are most likely to buy a long-term or subscription plan to a service when they desperately need it. The two aforementioned examples are a case in point. This might be true of most countries too, but more so of India, where we refuse to accept the urgency of a situation unless it hits us in the face. Other nationalities are more circumspect. For example, my German friend Stefan (name changed) has an insurance plan for a rather unlikely situation. If he gets stuck on an island, a helicopter will fly and pick him up at a minimal cost. Stefan knows that 99 per cent he will not need this insurance plan. But if at all he needs, he would not have to pay an astronomical amount.

On the contrary, I am not sure if Indians would even consider buying car insurance if it was not mandatory. The fear of being caught by traffic police drives them to buy one. Contrast this with the attitude to long-term savings. With no social security provisions such as state-sponsored pensions, most Indians in middle- and high-income groups save up for their retirement voluntarily.

According to a report by the Aegon Center for Longevity and Retirement, titled *The New Social Contract: A Blueprint for Retirement in the 21st Century*, India leads the way in retirement readiness among fifteen countries surveyed across Europe, America, Asia and Australia. The survey was conducted among middle- and high-income individuals. 'A combination of shorter careers, lack of social security, nuclear families becoming more common, which means reduced dependence on children, increasing life expectancy is pushing Indians to focus more and more on retirement,' said Vishal Dhawan, a certified financial planner and founder of Plan Ahead Wealth Advisors, a financial planning firm, in an article published in the *Mint*.[1] India is the only country to score more than 7.3 on the Aegon Retirement Readiness Index (ARRI) against a global average of 5.9. As much as 55 per cent of working people in India are saving for retirement regularly compared to 39 per cent globally.[2]

We love to save and hate to spend, especially on things that don't give instant gratification. Wait, there is more. We also have a relationship with negotiation.

India is a beautifully chaotic country and we love to negotiate regardless of whether we are buying or selling. In fact, we negotiate in our personal lives and relationships every day. We have mastered that art. Till the age of twenty-three, I negotiated my curfew time with my parents every time I went out for dinner with friends. Couples negotiate their living situations when they get married: should we live with the family or on our own? Sometimes they even negotiate with their parents on subjects concerning their future partners: who, how and when. Their families negotiate the expense of the infamous big fat Indian wedding. We know how to deal with pricing, and it can be tough to convince us to pay for something which we don't see of much value. Hence, it is safe to say that one of the most challenging business decisions for a start-up in India is pricing. This book tells the stories of entrepreneurs who were not dependent on heavy VC money to deal with their pricing but rather competed with heavily funded start-ups and figured out their pricing. However, whether or not you are VC-backed, these hacks are still applicable.

Relationship between Price and Product: The Biryani Rule

Price connects directly to business revenues and also defines the value perception associated with the product. The importance of knowing what your product is going to be used for by the client is *the* most critical question, according to Vishal Mehta of Infibeam. Infibeam is one of the bootstrapped unicorns of India that eventually got listed on the national exchanges. It is an internet and e-commerce conglomerate involved in digital payments, online retailing, e-commerce software and internet services.

To explain the biryani rule, let's take a scenario in which biryani (the famous Indian rice dish) is the end product and your product is the rice that is required to make the biryani. If you are the rice provider, you need to know whether your client is going to use your rice to make the biryani. Biryani requires the basmati variety of rice, which is more expensive than regular rice. If you know the real worth of exotic biryani, you will not price the rice at ₹5 per kilogram, which is too low. That's because the biryani will be sold at over 10x that price. You need to know what your client is going to do with the framework, the potential of that end product and how much it can be scaled up. That is when you will realise that you are not selling a product but a solution.

'Additionally, you have to figure out what other value-added solutions you can offer them so that they can sell it for ₹50. If you don't know what they want to do with your solution then you will never be able to add value to them,' noted Mehta.

Value-Based Pricing

While value-based pricing is the most popular among entrepreneurs and investors, Paras Chopra of Wingify drew from his experience to say that in today's world customers don't necessarily pay for the value but rather pay for what they think is fair. Business customers have expectations about the price of products or services depending on their experiences. If a company were to offer a B2B product or service for free, the customer will expect the product or service to be inexpensive and appropriate for small businesses. Similarly, if it charges $5,000 per month, they will expect personalised attention and dedicated customer service representatives.

The pricing game requires strategy, and Paras Chopra has learned some lessons on pricing in the B2B world. He wrote in his blog,

> I'll give an example. Pricing for [Visual Website Optimizer] VWO (Wingify's first product) started from $49 per month, and the highest plan we showed on the website was $249 per month. By doing this, we were telling the customer that we're meant for mid-sized businesses. Even though our product created value for enterprises and small businesses, we were excluding them because that's a price these two types of customers weren't familiar with in their previous purchases. Economic theory suggests that if an enterprise comes across $49 per month service that generates 100x value, it's a steal, but in my experience, enterprises do not go for cheap products because the price means the product isn't for them.

But what do you do if your first customer is unwilling to pay the quoted amount? Infibeam's Mehta was offered only ₹50,000 (approx $600 at 2023 rate) for the first product he built. He had no choice but to accept the offer because they had no other inflow of cash. His advice is simple: try your best to change the value but take whatever you get initially. As an entrepreneur, Mehta believed that it was better to take ₹50,000 initially, even though he wasn't completely satisfied with it, and reinvest it in building the product. This is to be done in such a way that you and your product are taken seriously. Funded start-ups, on the other hand, have the option to offer their products for free; they might though find it relatively more challenging to know how much the customers want to pay.

However, once the platform was tested, Mehta was clear they were going to take a large retailer as their first customer and not the smaller ones because doing so will cover all use cases of their product, just as my cleaning lady did. Sumeetra wanted to show others that she already had a few clients. Also, she wanted a recurring income over a one-time payment, as in the longer run, that's in her interest. If you look at global trends, even big companies such as Adobe and Microsoft no longer sell their software at eye-watering prices. Instead, both these companies have a subscription model, where you pay a fraction of the cost to use Adobe Creative Cloud or Microsoft Office. These subscriptions may even cost less than what they used to cost in the past when buying the software outrightly. But with a recurring subscription fee, both the software giants have well-oiled revenue-generating machinery.

There is always confusion as to whether one should charge the first few customers of a product. Let's see with an example. Remember when the goods and services tax (GST) law was passed in India? GST is a unified indirect tax that has replaced many indirect taxes. The law came into effect on 1 July 2017. In simple words, it is an indirect tax levied on the supply of goods and services. You cannot escape GST if you run a company or provide goods and services. When it became law, there was a lot of confusion on how to file for it and claim credits against it. The need for a software-based solution for GST filing was felt across the board. Everyone needed it.

Clearing the Web

ClearTax, a company listed in the 'Top 50 Start-ups That May Be the Next Unicorn' by CB Insights and featured in the *New York Times* in 2018,[3] had a product completely focused on India and probably the first one to launch a GST product in the country. An ex-employee of ClearTax said there were many reasons why they could charge a price for services at that time when the GST law was introduced in the country. He said,

> If we had a price attached to it, we knew that people would not just subscribe to the product but also use it. No one pays for something and then never use it. The second reason why we wanted people to pay was price discovery. No one knew about the price of such a service because till now such queries were handled by individual chartered accountants. We wanted to discover the price with our own analysis. Our technical team was solid, but we had no idea how to price the product. We wanted to see whether a large enterprise would pay for something like this? The competition was either charging very high or very low. There was a requirement for product validation and to find a product–market fit.

The product was brought into the market before it became fully functional, and that too at a price. The question was who would be its target customers.

There are three kinds of customers. First, those who use a product for free, but their intent is not clear. Second, those who use a product once for free but do not convert. Third, those who use a product with a clear intent of buying it. When the GST law came, all these three types of customers were potential converts. This is similar to how we all needed Paytm when demonetisation happened. We needed digital wallets because we were out of cash. Urgency can give birth to unicorns in India.

Changing the Habit of 'Free' Is Tough

Unless a necessity like GST presents itself, it can be difficult to nudge customers away from the habit of receiving a 'free' product. According to a blog authored by Paras Chopra (2017), customers often tend to judge the value of innovative products based on existing categories, which may not accurately reflect their true potential. This was evident from the experiences of Wingify in which two different products faced similar challenges. The first product, called in3bullets, provided daily summaries of long-form articles through a newsletter. During the beta phase, users expressed satisfaction and developed a habit of using the service. However, when Wingify decided to charge for the service, very few beta users were willing to pay. This unexpected response indicated that users perceived the fair price for such a service to be zero, influenced by the expectation of free information on the internet. Similarly, Wingify faced a similar issue with another product experiment. This product was a digital art frame that displayed a new piece of art every day. While beta users initially liked the product, they questioned its differentiation from a regular monitor with a slideshow. It became clear that customers automatically compared the product to familiar alternatives, leading them to perceive its value based on previous experiences rather than recognising its unique economic value.

In essence, the challenge lies in effectively positioning innovative products to ensure that customers understand and appreciate their true value instead of comparing them to existing categories. This becomes particularly challenging in a digital age where people have grown accustomed to accessing information for free, making it difficult to shift their expectations regarding pricing.

However, when a start-up is young, pricing strategies can be more flexible. Sridharan of Flexiple believes that pricing should be flexible and ought to be aligned with clients' ability to pay:

> That's the thesis we started off with. Initially, we benchmarked our markup against the other competitors in the industry. We

> started off with what Upwork charged, which was 20 per cent as a markup. But we also recognised that we provided a lot more value than Upwork. Not just because we're a competitor in the space but we actually did a lot more vetting. We provided much more support, made proper recommendations and so on. So we felt that we deserved a higher commission. We wanted to reach that golden number. That's what a lot of start-ups try to do. But then we realised we don't really need to have a fixed number. We can just talk to clients and freelancers and figure out what that number is on the go. And we let it be subjective.

As an independent journalist, I looked at the following funnels for my own pricing:

- Determine your free material: One of the first steps is to determine what you are willing to give away for free. When I started my career as a writer, this was an option, but not any more. Who does not like a story published in a national daily as a young journalism graduate looking for a job even when it does not pay? It is a stage when entering the journalism world was more important than getting paid. Young start-ups do this at the testing stage of their products when they are hungry for feedback.
- Finding the sweet spot: Now, let's talk about the 'bliss point'. It's like when food tastes so good that you can't get enough of it. Well, in our case, it's about delivering such fantastic work that people can't resist coming back for more. So, when you start charging for your writing, offer your first piece at a slightly lower price (70 per cent of your regular rate) but make sure it's still top-notch quality. This way, you'll impress your clients, and they'll be willing to pay more in the future.
- Scaling up: As you establish yourself, it's time to offer bigger and more valuable products or services. For

example, you can create training programmes on business journalism and writing. These programmes allow people to learn from your expertise without needing individual attention. It's like sharing your knowledge with a larger audience and helping them overcome complicated problems.

- The pinnacle: Eventually, you reach the highest level. People recognise your skill and reputation, and they want to hire you personally for one-on-one work. However, because you've built your business successfully, your services come at a higher price. This is important because being too cheap would lead to excessive demand and burnout. By charging a premium, you can provide excellent service while maintaining a healthy work–life balance.

The number of potential buyers for your product will vary depending on the level of interest in the product and the intent to buy. There will be customers who love the product but are looking for customisation. These are the ones who buy the product and then come back with recommendations to make it customisable to their needs. They are then liable to be charged for. The intent of the product then is to capture new markets while retaining customers for the long term.

B2B vs B2C Pricing

You must have come across different pricing strategies such as competition-based pricing, cost-plus pricing, dynamic pricing, freemium pricing, high-low pricing, hourly pricing, skimming pricing, penetration pricing, premium pricing, project-based pricing or value-based pricing when you read white papers on what pricing strategy to follow. However, many times the question really is whether to charge or not, which has been dealt with in the previous section.

Rahul Khanna of Trifecta Capital shared the same sentiment when he said, 'I think that in a B2B business, there is probably a slightly more nuanced view to saying that people are fundamentally used to price by capacity.'

This can be best explained with an example. Imagine you have two entrepreneurs, Alex and Emma, who both decide to start their own lemonade businesses. Alex plans to sell lemonade to other businesses, while Emma wants to sell lemonade directly to consumers.

Let's explore how they approach pricing:

B2B Pricing (Alex's adventure): Alex focuses on selling his delicious lemonade to other businesses. He knows that businesses have unique needs and considerations when it comes to purchasing supplies for their employees or customers. So, Alex carefully considers the following factors in his pricing strategy:

- ✦ Bulk orders: Since businesses typically need larger quantities of lemonade, Alex offers discounted prices for bulk orders. This makes it more enticing for businesses to purchase from him rather than his competitors.
- ✦ Long-term contracts: Alex recognises that businesses prefer long-term partnerships. He offers discounted prices or exclusive deals to businesses that commit to purchasing his lemonade for an extended period. This way, he can secure steady business and build lasting relationships.
- ✦ Customisation and delivery: Alex understands that businesses may have specific requirements or preferences. He offers customisation options, such as different flavours or packaging sizes, to cater to their needs. Additionally, he provides efficient delivery

services to ensure the lemonade arrives on time and in good condition.

B2C Pricing (Emma's adventure): Emma, on the other hand, wants to sell her refreshing lemonade directly to consumers. She sets up a lemonade stand and attracts customers passing by. Emma takes a slightly different approach in her pricing strategy:

- Competitive pricing: Emma considers the prices of other lemonade stands in the area and aims to offer a competitive price. She wants her lemonade to be affordable and appealing to potential customers. By aligning with or offering a slightly lower price than her competitors, she can attract more customers.
- Small portions and add-ons: Emma offers different portion sizes to accommodate various preferences and budgets. She provides small-sized cups at a lower price point, making it an accessible option for those seeking a quick refreshment. Additionally, she offers optional add-ons like fruit slices or a fancy straw for a slightly higher price, appealing to customers who want a little something extra.
- Eye-catching promotions: Emma understands the power of attracting customers with eye-catching promotions. She might offer a 'buy one, get one free' deal or introduce a loyalty card system where customers receive a free lemonade after purchasing a certain number. These promotions create excitement and encourage repeat business.

By tailoring their pricing strategies to their target markets, both Alex and Emma maximise their chances of success. Alex focuses on accommodating the unique needs of businesses by offering bulk discounts, customisation and long-term contracts. Emma, on the other hand, aims to attract individual customers with competitive pricing, different portion sizes and enticing promotions at her lemonade stand.

In the end, their lemonade adventures demonstrate how understanding the specific demands and preferences of B2B and B2C customers is essential in setting the right prices and building thriving businesses.

Should You Increase or Decrease Price with Time?

When you start a business, most of the time you focus on solving one problem with one feature. Once you get more customers, you tend to add a broader spectrum of features to your product. Your product becomes more and more valuable to your customers. Inherently, you start providing a service. You build customer support and customer succession services, and all this involves cost. The job does not end after selling the product. It has to be good enough so that people are convinced to use it over a long period of time.

Sunil Patro, the founder of US-based start-up SignEasy, has a relatable example to share in this regard. SignEasy is a cloud-based solution to help users sign and fill documents or get documents signed on a phone, tablet or computer. SignEasy was launched at an introductory price of $3. People would download the app for free and then pay $3 for the service. Patro realised over a period of time that SignEasy was not just an app but a solution. When you are a service, you realise you have other costs such as customer support, infrastructure, sales and marketing. He said,

> There is a notion that there is something wrong if you are selling really cheap. So internally in the company, we had to talk hard

> about how it is helping businesses – saving time, getting higher conversions of customers and helping admins stay on top of their paperwork. You have to constantly think about how you are building something of value, so it is important to price it in a way that the company runs profitably and grows at the desired rate. If the value does not grow, the price can't grow.

Price and margins too have an intrinsic relationship. According to Divyank of Directi, as an entrepreneur or a start-up, if you are making crazy amounts of profit, your competitors will come and squeeze them out. One needs to make money on the scale, not on the growth margin. That way, no start-up can come and cut you on pricing.

Why Decrease Price? India Is a Volume Game

A high-low pricing strategy is when a company initially sells a product at a high price but lowers that price when the product drops in novelty or relevance. Discounts, clearance sections and year-end sales are examples of high-low pricing in action. This is contrary to Patro's strategy at SignEasy.

But for Zoho, unlike SignEasy, the pricing has never increased, mostly only decreased even though they are a SaaS company. They are in a very different business than what they started off in. 'In Zoho, we are in the volume game,' said Vembu. 'The principles always remain true such as viability, business fundamentals and accounting rules. Those don't change. But what changes are the industry landscape, the competition and that impacts pricing.'

Gamble with Price

Author Scott Adams said, 'The world is like a reverse casino. In a casino, if you gamble long enough, you're certainly going to lose. But in the real world, where the only thing you're gambling is, say, your time or your embarrassment, then the more stuff you do, the more you give luck a chance to find you.'

When a start-up decides its product pricing, adopting a mindset of experimentation, adaptation and embracing risks can increase the chances of finding the optimal pricing strategy. By actively exploring different approaches and adjusting based on feedback, start-ups give themselves more opportunities for success to find them, just as in a reverse casino where more gambling increases the chances of luck being in your favour.

Nithin Kamath pointed out two things that applied to his business. One, in a world where everything was going online and prices were dropping, percentage broking didn't make sense any more. Today if you go to a bank and buy shares worth ₹10,000, you pay ₹100 as a fee. You buy for ₹1 lakh and you pay ₹1,000. It is a percentage progression, but a traditional/physical bank doesn't put any extra effort into the larger trade.

To explain Zerodha's pricing strategy, Nithin Kamath said,

> Our business is not like an e-commerce website. If you bought ten TVs, I don't have to worry about the logistics of sending you those ten TVs. For me, it's still the same TV. When we started, we had a flat ₹20 per trade concept. The concept was that my cost is recovered at twenty bucks. That's all that matters to me. With online trading, people could save 90–95 per cent of the brokerage they were paying otherwise.

The second thing that Zerodha focused on was transparency in its operations. Before, financial service businesses around the world were quite opaque. It was impossible to know the exact interest rate that you pay on your credit card or home loan.

According to Nithin, Zerodha is the first to bring a brokerage calculator that showed all the charges even before you trade, so there was never a question about customers being charged more than they should be or without their knowledge. They ensured that they had one pricing for all. Today, people are categorised based on how much they earn and how much money they have in their bank accounts. That's how people have been treated by their banks. Zerodha worked on levelling the playing field.

'Generally, in India, we have this attitude where shit doesn't stink because we have been treated like this forever by our banks,' said Nithin. 'We actually started vlogging about everything that was happening in the market. We were probably the first guys in financial services who put everything out on a vlog, and I even started an outreach programme. All this became immensely popular.' For Zerodha, a person with ₹1 lakh and another with ₹100 crore are the same, so they started offering a single deal to all their clients in every possible way, right from account opening cost to any other services they provided.

When competition started kicking in, Nithin realised he could not be just a low-cost, transparent guy who vlogs about everything any more. He said, 'In the third year, it was time to focus more on technology, and looking back today, I feel I probably should have done that right from the start. It shouldn't have taken me two years to figure that out.'

Then one fine day, suddenly, Nithin decided to play the casino gamble. Zerodha went zero on brokerage fees. Yes, you read it right! Starting 1 December 2015, all investments on Zerodha became absolutely free. No upfront fees, no minimum volume, no special terms and conditions, no clauses and no strings attached.

In a blog after that, Nithin wrote, 'Right from the conception of our name, the plan was to get here. It has taken us over five years. This wasn't done on the back of any VC/PE fundraise nor do we have any such plans for the near future.'

Why did Nithin decide to go zero brokerage suddenly? As a business, Zerodha soon realised how shallow the stock market participation was in India, probably not more than a million active investors (less than 0.1 per cent of the population). Just as for brokerage businesses such as Zerodha, the economic growth of modern India hinges on vibrant capital markets. 'Sixty-five per cent of the Indian population is below the age of thirty-five, and something has to be done to attract them to start investing in the markets. For this to happen, I think we need to bring coolness into the brokerage business,' said Nithin. With Kite (Zerodha's yet-to-be-launched mobile app at that time) the focus was to make the user interface clutter-free and as less intimidating as possible for a new investor (read user) while still being able to give all the power in terms of speed, charting and functionality that an active trader needs. At the time the offer was being made, Nithin said,

> In essence, investment culture has to be nurtured, and we intend to do this not just by offering a zero-brokerage investing platform, but also extremely easy user experience. The plan is to onboard the next one million participants who are currently not investing, show them how the stock market can create wealth if invested for the long term, help grow the capital markets in India and also hope that a few of them will turn traders and add revenue to our business.

However, the zero-brokerage offer on equity delivery trades was applicable only to retail investors. Corporates, partnerships, HUFs and other institutions had to continue to pay 0.1 per cent or ₹20 per executed order, whichever is lower.

The zero-brokerage decision might sound random now, but Zerodha had been planning on this for a while.

'At zero brokerage, we got so many eyeballs it's not even funny,' Nithin said. It took Zerodha the first three and a half years to get to their first ten thousand customers. Sometimes, starting with freebies is not the best idea, but, like Zerodha, playing the casino gamble to try your luck in the middle of the game could get you the next wave of new customers.

But then the question arises: how do you compete with funded players? According to Nithin, the answer lies in 'economies of scale' and first-mover advantage. 'When I see my competitors who have a thousand to two thousand clients, they will not have enough money to spend the way I do. And I don't think there is anyone out there who is going to fund them unless they come up with some technological advancement and a customer base as mine,' Nithin said in 2017. The margins have stayed for Zerodha because they have been able to add so much more business, and the scale has gone up significantly.

Scalability of Pricing Strategy and Business Model

In India, the time horizon to get profitable is not one or two years like in Silicon Valley. Companies have to put in a lot more rigour, a lot more processes and a lot more systems. When Infibeam started operations in India towards the end of 2007, the e-commerce industry was just emerging and growing. But Mehta's philosophy is to keep on scaling up. They signed up clients, but they also lost some. Over a period of time, he realised two things about India. First, in B2C e-commerce, even with all the data you have today, if you acquire a customer by losing money, you will never make money out of that customer. You can't acquire a customer by losing money at the gross margin level. Second, you have to figure out how to offer a workable solution to your customers.

For example, let's say you launch something at a certain price, say, 'x', and you are unable to sell at 'x' price in the initial days and your sales targets are much higher than what you are able to sell. In a country like India, if you try to collect feedback on why your product is not selling, the first response will be that the price is too high. Then, people will tell you there are other alternatives, some way cheaper. The instant reaction of most Indian entrepreneurs will be to try and reduce the price to match consumers' expectations.

Mehta dealt with a similar kind of situation at Infibeam. He said,

> The key over here is to actually go and talk to twenty consumers yourself and figure out whether you are able to communicate the advantages and benefits of the products. And if you're able to convert at least ten of them, then you know you're going to have a shot. But it takes that extra effort to do it because you have to train people on how to talk to users.

The first thing that Infibeam realised internally was that if you acquire a customer at a loss (not a net loss, we are talking about gross margin loss where you buy a product at ₹100 and sell it at ₹98), you will not make money from that customer because the customer came to you realising that this discount is business as usual for you. The second drawback of such crazy discounts is that if you scale up based on these discounts, there's no business model. You will have no option but to compound your losses.

According to Mehta, his start-up was losing customers in the initial days as there was no clarity on how to price the product. Over the years, through experimentation and testing various theses, he arrived at the conclusion that a business model should drive the product and technology, not the other way around.

'But business models only come with experimenting,' Mehta said. 'As an entrepreneur, one has to think hard about the thesis which should revolve around the business model. This is critical. One shouldn't assume that just because a business model worked in one region, it will work elsewhere. Consumers everywhere are different.'

He went with the thesis that his company could lose money while acquiring customers, and through these customers, it would eventually make money by offering value-added services over and above the regular service.

'But then you look at the data and you say, no, you can't do this immediately. You start realising that your thesis is wrong. So what is the next thesis and how do you architect your business model so that it starts working?' said Mehta, realising that a retailer spends most of his capital and money on only two things: technology and marketing. He then thought of increasing the cost of technology and making it scaleable. In line with this realisation, he changed his thesis. As Infibeam scaled up, it needed to make money. The money being made was then used as a forward investment to make more money.

Investing in a pricing approach has to be an investment in returns. Also, scalability impacts pricing, and in the internet world, scaling is not an option but a necessity.

Infibeam didn't want to work like Oracle or SAP, which give software and data, while the database is owned by their clients. Infibeam wanted to co-own the data since they were not in the business of selling data. The idea was to feed the data into its machine learning and deep learning frameworks so that Infibeam's system could learn. Their earlier business model, which was linked to variable costing and payment upon conversion method, did not work. It started off with clients paying a few lakh rupees a month and then moving out because the alternative for them was that somebody else was always willing to give them the software at a much lower price. Unfortunately, the clients did not realise what worked.

The thumb rule is to decide your pricing strategy based on whether you want to earn a lot of money from a few clients or a little money from a lot of clients. As a start-up, you need to understand where the pricing power lies.

How They Did It in the Early Days

MakeMyTrip started offering guaranteed low-fare tickets in 2005. Before that there was no discount if customers bought tickets online. The prices online and offline were the same. People bought tickets online only because of the convenience it offered. MakeMyTrip never had a pricing card. It positioned itself as an intermediary between the supplier and the buyer. Only 7 per cent of the visitors buy tickets on the platform while 93 per cent check prices and leave, according to Kalra. 'Those 7 per cent are the ones we need to focus on,' he said.

Pricing should be used only for one reason, as per Kalra: to induce people to buy/try/change habits. For instance, if people are buying offline, tell them to buy online with a discount and make their habits change. At the time when MakeMyTrip was launched, Kalra said, travellers had not much choice if they were to approach a travel agent. They could buy tickets only between 10 am and 6 pm on workdays and no services were available over the weekend. Online ticket booking was ruled by travel agents as many Indians did not use the internet. In 2005, MakeMyTrip gave the customers of India the power to choose, and that is what people paid for. It gave them control. Even though they paid extra for the convenience of online booking, they still got lower-price options compared to travel agents. One year later, in 2006, MakeMyTrip ran into a price war with Goibibo. But in 2016, during our interaction, Kalra was circumspect about the price war. Price wars help no one and spoil the market. The acquisition of Goibibo, in 2016, by MakeMyTrip, worth $1.8 billion, saw the newly merged travel giant grab more than 60 per cent of the overall online travel market in India in 2017.

Sachin Bhatia, co-founder and former CMO, MakeMyTrip; and co-founder and former CEO, TrulyMadly, believes that you start making money when you realise your business can't always run on VC money. You will never think hard about the bottom line if you had a lot of VC money. 'We were not confident about charging customers because we were scared they would run away,' he said. 'Instead, we focused on advertising revenue. We went out to all the big brands, and because of the volume of information (data) we had, we could do some fine targeting. We started with advertising, and then over time, we realised customers will pay us.' By leveraging their customer data, the dating app started collaborating with brands to reach their target audience. For example, they tied up with lingerie brand Zivame, convincing them that their target audience could be reached through them.

We are living in a world where too many things are available for free, especially in the online world. We are spoilt for choice. The problem is not scarcity but abundance. So the questions that beg answering are these: first, what value are you giving to your consumers that they will choose your product over others even if it is for free? Second, what value are you adding to your product that is so good that your customers will be willing to pay for the product over other players?

4

Is There an Ideal Business Model?

Hard fact: 97.8 per cent value of innovations goes to imitators. This means, the most successful business models in the technology industry today are copied.

'Whatever you launch, people are going to copy it. If you're lucky, you will have one year. Otherwise, it gets copied in six months,' said Infibeam founder Vishal Mehta. To be practical, there is absolutely no harm in copying a business model or a product idea. Participating in the race to 'be the first' is completely futile. In the real world, there are no prizes for being the first to launch a title. The two greatest examples that bring home this point are the iPhone and Google. Neither was the iPhone the first smartphone to be launched nor was Google the first search engine. Yet, these two companies have redefined those very categories. Ultimately, it's only customers that matter. Honestly, it's a little tiring to hear, 'What new problems are you solving as a start-up?' In most start-up pitches, young founders make a case for a problem that no one cares about. More companies die because of a lack of customers than getting killed by competition.

As a writer, I too relate to what Mehta advocates. Most stories are retold every few months by newspapers, and most fiction plots are recycled by authors (there are only eight basic plots). Many Bollywood movies still have the airport scene where one distressed lover arrives panting, just in time to stop the significant other from leaving. They fall into each other's arms and everything gets resolved. Countless directors have done it to death and the audiences have been lapping it up; yet, every time, the scene manages to push the audience to the edge of their seats. Similarly, your start-up business idea may be a copy inspired by another by being simply late to the party, but it could still make a scintillating entry into the market.

Wingify's Paras Chopra discusses the idea of copied business models on his blog. When he started VWO (a part of Wingify),[1] it wasn't the first web A/B testing tool. Google Optimize was the first, but VWO's differentiation was in making A/B testing easy. Paras wrote in his blog,

> When I started Pushcrew, it wasn't the first web push notifications tool. OneSignal and Roost were already present in the market, but Pushcrew's differentiation was focused on the mid-market. In contrast, whenever I tried innovating, coming up with breakthrough products, they failed. We all know the iPhone wasn't the first smartphone neither was Google the first search engine nor Facebook the first social network. Of course, you know that being first in the market means little if you're in the wrong market.[2]

But how do you identify if you are copying things the right way and for the right market? Simply copying a US-based business model and pasting it in the Indian market will not work.

We are a country of clever customers. We are pampered by the overwhelming consumer market and we don't get easily convinced to do things unless it is a norm for all citizens. We would not bother to buy a subway/metro ticket if there were no sensors installed at the gates. We would not pay taxes on time if not for the late fine. We would not feel guilty about saving our money wherever we can by avoiding these norms. We grew up in families where we were always taught to save for rainy days because we never had the option to reach out to the government for help or subsidies if we lost our job or were unemployed because of unavoidable reasons. Designing a business model for the Indian market isn't child's play. Here, the focus must be on making money even as your customers try to save some.

Keeping an Eye on Competitors' Business Model

For Karthik Sridharan, competition in the market is not a problem nor should it be a deterrent. Competitors validate your ideas. They establish the fact that there is adequate space for a start-up in the segment. But is there enough space for multiple such companies to coexist? Sridharan thinks there is:

> I felt that the market I was looking at – technology development and technology design – was really huge. The appetite of start-ups to hire such people is only going to grow multi-fold year after year. So we felt that such companies could successfully coexist in the market, and could all be successful. On the positive side, there can be a lot of things that you can learn from competition and actually leapfrog a lot of the initial stages of mistakes. To be honest, I've learned a lot from our competitors.
>
> Copying various aspects of your competitor's marketing is helpful. I've built a product. Now, how do I distribute it? How do I get it in front of customers? At the start, that used to be a very big question. And unless you have a competitor that's actually already doing that, it is really tough for you to have an exact intuition on what will work other than actually just going and trying it.

If you want to know how your competition is using, for example, Google and SEO to grow their marketing, you can analyse all the keywords and their rankings. It will give you an idea of how your competition is using paid advertising to grow their businesses. You might also want to know all their traffic sources. Once you have analysed all of those aspects, you will begin to understand the channels that could work for you, and then you can bring your own unique perspective on how you're going to be using those channels.

'Even in terms of messaging, I think it allows you to bring your unique way of identifying the gaps that your competition isn't fulfilling. You then need to figure out how your start-up can become the smarter alternative,' Sridharan added. 'Basically, with an established competitor, you have a benchmark against which people can actually measure you. There are these levers that you can use to actually showcase and get your first customers going and get a narrative out there.'

B2C vs B2B Business Models

The question I asked almost every entrepreneur and investor when I was trying to understand start-up business models was this: would you give the same advice to a person running a B2B company versus a B2C company? The line between B2B and B2C is getting blurred in many cases. I am not sure if a typical B2C model can survive in India without heavy VC funding, but a B2B model definitely could. This could be precisely why most business models pivot from B2C to B2B eventually. The simple reason could be that consumers or individuals don't want to spend money but businesses are relatively more open to spend on a product they believe will eventually bring higher profits. When it comes to B2C brands, usually there is only one that dominates the market. If our friends watch

Game of Thrones, we want to watch it too. And if they pick an iPhone over an Android or a pair of Levi's jeans over a Lee or Uber over Ola, we want to do the same. The grip of peer pressure and FOMO is real and relentless, and B2C businesses understand this human psychology well.

The most important thing to consider when you draw up your business model is the revenue: where is it going to be coming from? In a lot of cases, companies do not make money with what they sell. Confused? Let me explain. Movie theatres don't make money by selling tickets for movies. Their aim is to bring customers into theatres by paying for a ticket and then to get them to spend on popcorn, cold drinks and other ancillary services. A company selling printers will price the printers low as their real business is not just selling printers but also proprietary ink cartridges. Similarly, there are numerous business models that do not depend on the core product to make money. Unlike a physical movie theatre, an online business has more options to diversify into different channels to feed its core business.

The printer industry provides another compelling example of generating revenue beyond the initial sale. Printer manufacturers often price their devices relatively low, sometimes even at a loss. Why? The answer lies in their strategy to make money from proprietary ink cartridges. By keeping the printer price affordable, manufacturers ensure a large user base, creating an ongoing demand for ink cartridges that are specifically designed for their printers. This 'razor and blades' approach allows companies to generate recurring revenue from customers who continue to purchase ink refills. The pricing of the ink cartridges themselves tends to be higher, compensating for the initial printer discount.

The advent of the internet has opened up new possibilities for entrepreneurs to diversify their revenue streams. Online marketplaces, such as Amazon and eBay, provide platforms where sellers can showcase their products to a vast customer base. While the primary revenue comes from transaction fees or commissions on sales, successful marketplaces leverage additional services to increase their income. For instance, they offer advertising options for sellers to boost visibility, premium subscription plans with added benefits or fulfilment services to handle storage and shipping logistics. By expanding their offerings and providing value-added services, online marketplaces create new revenue streams while supporting their core business model.

In the B2C space, the customer is the primary source of revenue; that is the only way companies generate profit. But there are two models here: the media model and the transactional model. Within the media model, you're either the *New York Times*, and therefore positioned as a premium product with an affinity to what really matters in terms of news, or you are about performance and giving lots of inventory, which people are pricing to the penny, for example, ScoopWhoop, which is an Indian internet media and news company that creates and curates India specific stories in different categories. Traditional advertisers may not necessarily go to ScoopWhoop, but lots of businesses who want heavy traffic will readily hop on to the platform. Within the transactional model, there's the affiliate model, such as Couponraja and Coupondunia, which are both coupon code providers and work with India's largest e-commerce merchants. They drive business to merchants, and within that, they can be paid either by a lead or on conversion. For instance, Policybazaar is an affiliate that leads customers to an insurance company's website and gets paid for the lead or a sale that entitles it to a brokerage commission.

Subscription revenues of certain companies that earlier offered only a one-time payment model have grown.

For companies operating in a purely digital space, there is increased pressure to have recurring revenue via the subscription model. For instance, Apple, which still generates a lot of revenue from the sale of its hardware products, has doubled down on subscription services as the hardware market matures. From under $5 billion around 2013, Apple's services now account for close to $20 billion.

This is to say that all business models are growing at a pace attractive to someone or the other in the playing field. What business model fits your company is not something anyone can tell you. Not books. Not writers. Not mentors. Your business model will evolve as you grow, adapting to the complexity of the market you operate in.

Wingify's Chopra wrote in his blog that many start-ups transition from a B2C to a B2B business model:

> In my conversations with other entrepreneurs, I've come across tens of start-ups that started with a B2C angle but eventually succeeded as a B2B company. Outside of my experience, famous examples include Slack, that started as a gaming company. VWO's competitor, Optimizely, started as a company that made math teaching apps for children. In my experience, it's far more common to pivot from B2C to B2B than the reverse. Why does that happen?[3]

As of 2020, seven of India's twenty-nine unicorns were in the B2B SaaS business. Rajan Anandan, managing director of Peak XV Partners, believes that the emergence of unicorns is the reason behind the growing popularity of B2B models in the country:

> You have three unicorns, all which were founded a decade ago. Freshworks was India's first SaaS unicorn of resolve. We don't know what the valuation is, but it was at least the venture-funded

> variety. Then we had Dhruva. And now we have a circus. We have several thousand SaaS companies in India now. And a lot of these companies actually get to revenue very quickly. Therefore, theoretically, you could bootstrap a SaaS company to get to a couple of million dollars of revenue on the consumer side. I think it depends a lot on what the business is. Is it a gaming business or an e-commerce business? Is it a content business? Google has fifty thousand web publishers on Google Display Network, and tens of thousands of them are profitable. They're very small publishers; they get on the internet and start writing or creating content through digital advertising.

To build a large business, one necessarily needs capital. The investor in Anandan believes that some businesses more than others require capital. He said,

> If you want to build a large business, whether it's a B2B business or a B2C business, I think it does require capital. Some businesses require a lot more capital than others. If you don't require a lot of capital, you could theoretically bootstrap your way to revenue and then eventually profitability. You could start accruing your cash flows and you start funnelling that into your start-up. But if you want to build a large business in a space that is inherently capital intensive, you could think about mobility, right? Ride hailing company is right in the mobility space that is a pretty capital-intensive business. E-commerce generates a capital-intensive business because initially you have to provide incentives to get your users and then you have to invest in logistics and infrastructure and customer service and all those kinds of things.

How Infibeam Built One-of-a-Kind E-commerce Business Model

How Infibeam's Vishal Mehta, the man who listed the first e-commerce company in India with a billion-dollar valuation, figured out his business model is a storied tale. After interviewing him in 2017, I asked myself if Infibeam will be remembered as the Amazon of India. Amazon was a name that came up many times in my conversation with Mehta. I don't know what will happen after a decade, but the truth is that Infibeam is not a household name at present like Amazon. Mehta might have copied Amazon's business model, but he modified it to suit the Indian market. He did not care about being the first in India to be a household name in e-commerce but definitely cared about being the first profitable and publicly listed e-commerce company in the country.

In 2017, everyone knew Flipkart, India's largest e-commerce company that Walmart acquired in 2018, but it is doubtful if anyone would know Infibeam. In fact, an NDTV journalist who interviewed Mehta in 2016 asked, 'Now that the IPO has opened and you are in the market, can you tell me what Infibeam actually does? What can I do on the website of Infibeam?' The journalist focused on the fact that while Flipkart and Snapdeal were well known, he has no idea who bought Infibeam.

This is not surprising as the same media celebrated Walmart's acquisition of a majority stake in India's largest e-retailer, Flipkart, for $16 billion. Facing competition from Jeff Bezos's Amazon in the US, the world's largest retailer acquired India's largest online retailer. This granted Walmart access to Asia's third-largest economy where it could not set up brick-and-mortar stores. One could call this the end of the first phase of India's e-commerce journey and the start of the second phase.

Ankur Bisen, a senior partner at Technopak, said in a Bloomberg Quint interview, 'The first phase was dominated by hyper competition, extreme growth and the battle for gaining market share at any cost. This also led to a lot of players betting on "wrong business models". In the second phase, we'll see a lot more focus on business models, integration and scale. And that is good for e-commerce.'[4]

Ironically, Mehta, an ex-employee of Amazon, never really focused on the wrong business model and knew the granularities of the Indian market from the beginning. One could argue that he did not build a pure consumer brand, but in the end, he built the most or rather only profitable e-commerce company with a successful IPO in India. Infibeam is unlike traditional e-commerce companies, which only act as a marketplace for commodities being sold on the platforms. Such companies are heavily dependent on user traffic to stay in business, and hence they keep spending towards customer acquisition or retention.

In a 2015 Livemint interview, Mehta talked about why Infibeam was not doing what Flipkart or Snapdeal were doing at that time. He said, 'Only about 11 per cent of India's internet users have shopped online, and that number still has a long way to go. Our strategy is to keep adding more merchants and provide them more value-added services.'[5] His aim was to get more and more merchants online rather than selling products at a hefty discount. He made money out of convincing merchants to come online.

Infibeam has metamorphosed into an online retail marketplace that sells products in various categories such as mobile, electronic, book, baby care product, toy, beauty care, movie, music, etc. It started out as an automobile portal in 2007 but later pivoted to online retailing.

Infibeam is also a SaaS solution provider to retailers as well as brands, both Indian and international. Mehta was clear of its modus operandi since the beginning: saving the cost of technology for its customer, both end consumers and businesses. With the help of technology, you either provide in-demand solutions to merchants and suppliers or solve something on the capacity side such as in logistics. Infibeam enabled businesses to sell online on the demand side, which is typically a merchant who wants to send an invoice to a customer. Unlike Flipkart and Snapdeal, Infibeam wanted to help merchants who were selling products directly to their users or across marketplaces but weren't doing it online yet. It built BuildaBazaar, a SaaS platform, so that businesses and merchants can sell online.

There was another problem Mehta identified. There were some brands that already had a distribution channel but were struggling to reach a certain segment of customers. Let's take the example of the traditional retail brand Amul, which has more than two hundred products. According to Mehta, the distribution channel of Amul at that time would efficiently carry the two products that sold well but not the universe of products:

> We said we will help you sell the products that don't sell and don't get carried by the existing distribution channels by connecting you to B2B channels. The same platform that we built for the demand side expanded onto the supply side. We called up brands and said, since you don't have a supply chain, I'll help you with the supply chain, and that started building our capacity on the supply side. We expanded through multiple languages, multiple logistics providers, integration points.

So, it was not necessarily an innovation in services that did the trick for Infibeam but a creative way of using existing platforms for different customers. 'We actually earn our own money by making it more variable and less fixed. In other words, upon your success, we take a cut of the transaction,' Mehta said.

Scaling a Business Isn't an Option but a Necessity

If you acquire a customer at a loss, you won't make money, and you will end up compounding your losses. If the idea of suffering a loss now is to make money in the future, then it is okay. However, Infibeam approached it differently. Mehta said,

> Our thesis was very clear from the beginning that you cannot turn an unpaid customer into a paid one. We also knew that scale is not an option in the internet world; it is compulsory. We don't want to work like an Oracle or an SAP, who say that I'll give you the software, and the data and the database is the client's own database. Infibeam offered to co-own all that data and said that they are not in the business of selling data but can put their own machine learning and deep learning frameworks in it so they can learn and the system can learn from it.

This approach is now open to debate since the question of ethics around data privacy and the unsolicited selling of user data has taken a whole new meaning.

To get around the tricky situation of data privacy, Infibeam created two segments within its business model: one is the e-commerce marketplace called Infibeam, where merchants sell directly on its platform without hefty discounts, and the second is the service-driven model BuildaBazaar, which provides cloud-based infrastructure services to SMEs. For the SaaS option, Infibeam provides its customers end-to-end IT backbone, marketing and logistics support and also a payment gateway facility for online sales. Already sixty-six thousand SME and MSME businesses have enrolled with BuildaBazaar. The big names include Imagica, Canon, Hidesign and more. This is how Infibeam's business model worked as it earned by way of monthly fees as well as commission per transaction.

There's a difference between having a product and looking for a business model versus having a business model and then building a product. The difference is clear.

Business models only come with experimenting. Infibeam could have also followed the crowd and acquired customers by losing money, but instead, as Mehta said,

> We brainstormed as to how does one architect a business model. We also started realising that most of the capital and the money is spent by a retailer on only two things: technology and marketing. Hence, I will definitely eat up the cost of technology and make it scaleable for them. This was the first objective. As far as marketing is concerned, I'll open up all channels for them. Our thesis was that as we scale up, we need to make money and we will forward investment. We are not shy of forwarding investments, but it still has to give us returns.

In 2023, the Infibeam model completely pivoted on a B2B company. It has always focused on being a digital organisation that can solve problems at scale. It started with various digital businesses and now is a provider of digital payment solutions (DPSs) and enterprise software platforms (ESPs) in India. As a global fintech company, it caters to diverse B2B clients, using a deep understanding of e-commerce and digital payments.

The B2B model often faces the problem of explaining the value of a product to the customers and probably has to be very innovative in doing so. Paras Chopra wrote in his blog,

> My mistake with Wingify marketing platform was asking people to invest their time in learning what Wingify platform is capable of when they've just started interacting with the product. I was essentially telling them: 'Hey, you don't know me and have all reasons to suspect that I'm overpromising, but please spend several minutes trying to understand what is going on in the product. Trust me, I know my product will deliver you value many times the cost of your time'. This didn't fly with people, and so for my second product (Visual Website Optimizer), I

> eliminated everything. In this iteration, all the customer could do was just one thing: enter the URL of her website.

If you look at Amazon, a bulk of its profit comes from web services and not retail, which is infrastructure as a platform, and Amazon never talks too much about those numbers. While Amazon may have online retail and other consumer-facing services and products, over 52 per cent of its operating income comes from Amazon Web Services (AWS), its cloud services platform.[6] As of 2021, AWS controlled 33 per cent of the global cloud-based market.[7] There is apparently no model in India other than that of Infibeam's that is similar to Amazon's, at least when Mehta started the company. Mehta said,

> It was important that we had a very clean structure. We wanted to be sure that we are compliant with every aspect of investment and thought of a long-term and sustainable and expanded business model. We had almost broken even in our early years, which gave us an appetite to take risks. We had a lot of compliance and governance in place beforehand, so whether it was a private investment or a public investment, we were ready for that. The hard part was for us to communicate what our business model is. Because back then, there was not even a Shopify, a company which offers infrastructure-as-a-platform services for the US and Canada. But they were also not listed then, and today they are worth about $4–5 billion.

Consumers or investors did not have the time or patience to understand the business model of Infibeam, but the amount of time Mehta spent trying to make people understand how the company operated was a 'time well spent' because it gave him some indications about how to think through the services, and also, every interaction with regards to Infibeam became an opportunity to learn. 'In retrospect, I think it was a very good call because you are first able to communicate to people what e-commerce is,' he said. 'Back then, nobody knew what was a forward investment in such companies, and there was lots of speculation about who was profitable and who was not profitable. But in the last couple of years, there's a lot more information, and then there's always this focus on the gross merchandise value (GMV).'

For Infibeam, GMV Was not Translating into Profitability

Surprisingly, Infibeam never focused on GMV. For Mehta, if GMV was not translating into profitability then it was a baseless business model. GMV is another way of calculating a company's gross revenue, which refers to the total sales volume in dollars over a given time period on an e-commerce site.[8] The GMV figure, which was commonly used in place of sales or revenue figures in the early days of e-commerce by businesses to measure the value of a company, has now become outdated. Mehta knew it was something that did not work for him even in the early days of e-commerce. 'Once we put payments, it makes sense to talk about GMV because every payment will translate into more money,' Mehta said. 'But short of a marketplace and it translating into the bottom line, how do you essentially think about it in that business model perspective? So we went through our own ordeal. Those were testing times, but I think those are also opportunities for you to grow up as a company.'

In terms of economics, GMV is a raw figure that doesn't offer much insight into the value of the items sold because it doesn't factor in any costs accrued by the retailer. Additionally, GMV doesn't include discounts or returns or the cost of keeping and storing an inventory before it's sold. There are a few ways to calculate GMV. The simplest formula for a retailer is to take the sales price charged to the customer and multiply it by the number of items sold.

In the vast realm of e-commerce, one company stands tall, an unparalleled force that has reshaped the retail landscape: Amazon. Its journey from a humble online bookstore to a global tech giant is a testament to its ability to adapt, innovate and anticipate the changing needs of customers. Its business model evolution can be described as follows.

From Books to Everything: The Early Days

In the early 1990s, Amazon emerged as a disruptor, challenging the traditional brick-and-mortar retail model by offering an extensive selection of books online. As the pages turned, Amazon's visionary founder, Jeff Bezos, recognised the potential for expansion beyond books. The company diversified its product offerings, venturing into electronics, clothing, home goods and countless other categories. Like a chameleon, Amazon adapted its business model to cater to the diverse desires of its growing customer base.

Unleashing the Cloud: AWS and Technological Dominance

Recognising the rising demand for cloud computing services, Amazon harnessed its own technology infrastructure to create AWS. This strategic move not only transformed the company's revenue streams but also positioned Amazon as a pioneering force in the cloud computing market. From start-ups to Fortune 500 companies, businesses flocked to AWS for its scaleable infrastructure.

Prime: A Paradigm Shift in Customer Experience

The inkling of a groundbreaking idea took shape within Amazon's halls: a membership programme that would revolutionise customer loyalty and shopping habits. Thus, Amazon Prime was born. With unlimited fast shipping, exclusive deals and access to a burgeoning library of digital content, Prime members were granted an all-access pass to Amazon's marketplace. This bold initiative cemented Amazon's commitment to customer satisfaction and cultivated an unbreakable bond with its loyal followers.

Diversification through Acquisition: Building an Empire

In the pursuit of growth and innovation, Amazon embarked on a series of strategic acquisitions which redefined the boundaries of its business model. From Zappos, the online shoe retailer known for its unparalleled customer service, to Whole Foods Market, the grocery chain that added a tangible presence to Amazon's virtual marketplace, each acquisition served as a stepping stone towards a broader market domination. With each new addition, Amazon's offerings expanded, capturing the imagination of consumers worldwide.

The Digital Revolution: Kindle, Prime Video and Beyond

With the rise of digital content consumption, Amazon recognised the need to captivate audiences beyond the realm of physical products. Enter Kindle, the revolutionary e-reader that allowed bookworms to carry an entire library in their hands. As the digital world beckoned, Amazon delved deeper, launching Prime Video, an immersive streaming platform that challenged the entertainment industry's status quo. With each new digital venture, Amazon further solidified its position as a formidable force in the ever-evolving digital landscape.

Today, many e-commerce companies understand platform services and what Infibeam does, but no one did when they started doing it in India. According to Mehta, this was a blessing in disguise:

> Everybody who was out there were of the opinion that platform services is not the business that they want to explore. Platform services are where the bulk of profits are. This is the space to be, but I suspect that the important part is to keep on doing what you as an entrepreneur think is right. Look at it globally. Every B2C company has a B2B company. Today, if you look across the world and pull up the top 20 companies including Amazon, you will find every company is profitable. Hence, in the world, every company is profitable, and only in India, you have internet companies that are not profitable. I think that's the first part. You need to have something that actually gives you your winning. You can invest in things that you think are maybe twenty years out. If you don't have those winnings, then you'll have to raise more capital. There is no other way out.

Every company needs to have a winning segment somewhere, which will allow it to keep ploughing back into the business or into what it thinks is right. If you don't have that, you'll have to keep raising more capital because there's no other option. When capital becomes oxygen, it's easy to get addicted. The more you consume, the more you want it. One needs to architect a business model and its cash cows from day zero.

'There are a few companies, exceptions, that have done very well in B2C and have made money. The classic case in this instance is a jewellery company. In other words, they would have made money [anyway] because they deal in diamond, which has high profit margins,' said Mehta.

A horizontal B2C model like Amazon is where you sell different product lines. If you go horizontal across those product lines and product categories, there is a requirement for B2B support. In vertical B2C, the focus is on a few product categories with high margins. In some verticals where you have a proprietary product, you have an advantage or an opportunity to monetise from it. Think of the iPhone. Its selling price is many times higher than its cost of production. These high margins have ensured that Apple rakes in profits. The margins in this type of model tend to be larger compared to what you would see in horizontal B2C. For a B2C to work well in a vertical set-up, it has to have an evolved ecosystem where there are many service providers.

The line between B2B and B2C is blurring quickly. Right now, you can think of a brand as a retailer or as just a brand. Apple, with its own stores, is a retailer as well as a brand. Earlier, Apple would go to its distributor Ingram Micro, and Ingram Micro would in turn go to a sub-distributor and then to a retailer. Now, Ingram Micro deals directly with retailers. It wouldn't be a surprise if Ingram Micro starts billing directly. This arrangement between Apple and Ingram Micro went on for many years. Apple began selling directly to customers via its website only since 2020.[9]

Coming back to Rahul Khanna, who was trying to explain various business models, he does not necessarily feel that Infibeam is a bootstrapped success. According to him, if you're using your own money to fund a business, it's not bootstrapping:

> Infibeam didn't get built for free. To me, bootstrapping is really when you're building a business where your actual costs are very low and you did not fund it externally or internally. I guess Infibeam has done a great job of not throwing money away. So if Infibeam thinks that getting to scale and getting to IPO was the outcome they wanted, they got there, and maybe they've created a lot of value for themselves. But is it sustainable? Do customers really want to shop on Infibeam? Is there really a loyalty that they've created? What is success and over what time frame do you measure it? As a founder of Infibeam, I'm sure he is very happy. The company's done well, and from their standpoint, they haven't got infinite degree of freedom to do whatever they want to do, different from guys who've raised funds from VCs. So it depends on what you're solving for.

I am no one to decide whether Infibeam is better than Flipkart or vice versa. In one case, the success of the entrepreneur is not linked to the individuality of the start-up. On the other, the two identities are strongly linked. Despite being the founders of Flipkart, Sachin Bansal and Binny Bansal had a dramatic exit when Walmart acquired it. While Sachin exited just after the acquisition was announced, Binny was asked to resign a few months later due to 'personal misconduct', according to media reports. On the other hand, it is hard to imagine what would Infibeam be like without Mehta's business model. No one knows what tomorrow will bring, but during my conversation with Mehta, he did not, even for a moment, demonstrate that he was going to sell Infibeam or exit fully in the future.

The sense I get while talking to founders of bootstrapped start-ups is this: their destination is not exit. It is a goal much bigger than that. Zoho's Vembu wrote in his blog in 2011:

> That crazy idea, directly funding infrastructure out of profit, would practically get me thrown out of my job in a nanosecond if Zoho were a public company. That is why I don't take venture capital and won't ever take my company public. The good news is we have decent profit, and as we grow, my plan is increasingly becoming less and less crazy. But it is not really about me. I live the good life. It is my employees in Chennai that are the true heroes. Every single one of them go to work under these [tough] conditions – and I am going to be there tomorrow. Our people write code, support customers, teach and learn from each other, all under these conditions. The fact that our people ship the products they do under these conditions is a testimony to the resilience of the human spirit. I grew up in exactly these circumstances, but I still think of it as nothing less than a miracle that we are able to do the work we do.

It is a work of deep perseverance to build a company that's going to last decades. A founder like Bill Gates and a company like Microsoft are rare. The Flipkart acquisition by Walmart shows that the people at Flipkart had been building something that was only going to fill a gap for a big company like Walmart to enter the Indian market. Would Flipkart have competed with China's Alibaba if the latter had sought to acquire the former but gotten rebuffed instead?

India celebrated the $16 billion acquisition of Flipkart by Walmart in May 2018. The grand spectacle suggested to me that the chances of a Bill Gates emerging from India has become lesser than ever. It will become impossible now for a founder to nurture a start-up and build a behemoth yet braving all odds and sticking by it. The IT sector has seen stories of Infosys and its co-founder Narayan Murthy not letting IBM take over the flourishing IT services sector in India. What is the business model that Indian start-ups need to crack so that one day we will have an Amazon or an Alibaba or an Uber from India? What Infibeam is doing might not be glamorous enough to be labelled as the poster boy of Indian start-up or be covered frequently by the media, but it is definitely a business model that makes you ask, 'What is your definition of success?'

5

Narcissism, Depression and Burnout in the Indian Start-up Ecosystem

Don't f*** with my baby,' thundered the thirty-five-year-old founder, her eyes red with emotion. She sat across the table in the office meeting room, yelling at me one-on-one. It seemed like her world had shattered and no one else could understand her pain. She was fulminating at an intern for a minor spelling mistake in a product launch post on the company's Instagram page. The mistake, which was corrected in precisely thirty seconds, had caught her eyes. For someone like me, who has worked in high-pressure newsrooms and handled crisis situations in multinational companies, this seemed like an extreme reaction. The experience I had that day sitting on that table alone in a meeting room with the founder made me realise the amount of stress, delusion and mental trauma entrepreneurs face. Unfortunately, that is exactly how toxic culture flows from the top to an employee like me who manages a team and then down to the interns.

If you were to ask me five years back, I would have never considered writing this chapter. Until I met business founders who were responsible for toxic work culture, I thought that company culture is overrated. People will work hard and get things done if they have to or are self-motivated. I felt that people in any organisation are always replaceable, and that statement still stands true.

Unfortunately, the only irreplaceable person in a team is the founder, and they can make or break a company. They can turn a self-motivated and ambitious employee into a low performer. Such a person will never become a leader that every single person in the company would like to work with. Before I delve deeper into the characteristics of start-up founders, there is something that needs more attention: the voice of the employees, especially in the Indian context.

Depression and Burnout: The Darkest Side of Indian Start-up Scene

My friend Arpit, whose name appears a few times in the book, has been a quintessential employee of the Indian start-up ecosystem. His phone rings even at midnight if his employers are stressed about something. Vacations with him would always include work calls. He would disappear for days due to work and suddenly appear in, say, Bali (on Instagram) on a vacation. After a few years of working at C-level positions in top VC-funded start-ups, he decided to either work on his own start-up idea or bring some balance to his work–life. Often when we sit down to have conversations about what passion means, some way or the other, we would always drift back to work, success and doing something *big*. For him, specifically, creating his start-up, his baby, his own idea, was at the top, which, whatever it is, I'm sure will be something phenomenal to talk about today.

What happens when so much passion is put into building a start-up and ensuring it is successful, especially in a country like India? As kids growing up in India, we were taught that being a rank holder in school is what defines success. To be better than everyone and to be ahead of others is success. Just run, run and run so that no one catches up with you.

For start-up founders, their identity among their family, friends and professional circles is related to the success of their start-ups. Nothing else matters.

And when they fail, sometimes the price is very high. In 2019, Veerappa Gangaiah Siddhartha Hegde, the CEO of India's most prominent homegrown coffee chain Cafe Coffee Day, committed suicide.

Is making a business profitable such a big dream that if it does not get fulfilled you would kill yourself? Why did Hegde think of it as the only option? Why was he not able to open up to his friends, family or investors? In spite of such tragic incidents, why don't we still talk openly about depression in the Indian start-up scene?

Hegde's letter was trenchant with his observation of the alleged failure of the system to support a well-meaning entrepreneur.

Why don't we have a mental health clause in term sheets created by investors? Why is it such a taboo?

In 2020, Rachit Gupta, now in the Peak XV Partners investment team, opened up on Twitter about depression and failure:

FIG 5.1 While many start-up founders suffer from depression, talking about mental health is considered a taboo

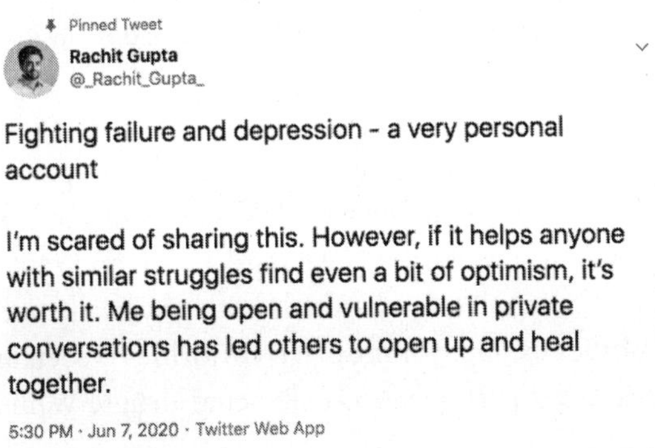

Gupta further wrote, 'In 2017, I had just shut down my second start-up. Nearly broke, burnt out, with no plans. Mentally, I was depressed, with a complete lack of self-confidence and self-worth. Had I wasted four years of prime youth? I took career failure very, very personally. It wasn't my first bout of depression, but it was the most severe.'[1]

What Can VC Money Do to Company Culture?

Do companies that don't need to constantly prove themselves to investors tend to have happier employees, better mental health and founders who have a clearer sense of their own identity?

For Vembu of Zoho, a farming analogy explains this situation perfectly:

> The VC model tends to be like highly chemical-intensive farming where you first use fertilisers and pesticides and then you grow fast and then you harvest. Harvest is the exit, while bootstrapping is a more sustainable eco-agriculture. With bootstrapping, initially it will be slower and you won't achieve rapid growth rates like those VC models, but it's likely to prove more durable. The soil retains its fertility. One of the problems that you have in chemical-intensive farming is topsoil erosion; the topsoil in the company case would be the culture of the company, so VC companies tend to lose their culture.

Sometimes, we may perceive someone as being unstoppable, but over a period of ten to fifteen years, the company culture can suffer due to the pressures of seeking VC exit and rapid growth. This takes a toll on individuals both physically and mentally. Another example of misplaced priorities is seen in sportspersons using performance-enhancing drugs. While they may achieve short-term success and win medals early on, these drugs can be harmful in the long run, catching up with them in their forties and fifties. Running a business is not a sprint, it's more like participating in a lifelong marathon.

This is backed by the experience of Wingify's Chopra. 'We celebrate hyper growth all the time, and so for a young person, it is very hard to resist the lure of hyper growth,' he said. 'There is some magical thing about hyper growth, like you go from zero to a billion dollars in five or eight years or something. It appears magical and a lot of people want to chase it, but it comes at a cost.'

It was only in 2020 that business founders started talking publicly about therapy and mental distress in India. Piyush Kumar, co-founder and CEO of the Indian start-up Rooter, started going to therapy in May 2020 and spoke openly about it in an article in Business Insider.[2] During the COVID-19 pandemic, Kumar had to work eighteen to twenty hours a day, ensuring smooth transitions for his team to working from home. Kumar was simultaneously working on a product for Rooter. His top priority was to turn a recently signed term sheet into an investment.

What Needs to Change?

Long working hours are not uncommon in India, but there is something we need to be worried about: mental health. In an article published in Quartz[3] in 2020, at least ten start-up employees from across the country described their experience in the workplace as 'chaotic' and 'messy'. They felt stifled at work and were desperate for alternative opportunities. A LinkedIn list of the top twenty-five start-ups in the country revealed an encouraging trend that thriving start-ups have managed to lure talents away from established companies with worker-friendly incentives.[4] For instance, Cure.fit, a health and wellness company that ranked second on the list, promised employees a flat hierarchy, flexible working hours and the freedom to choose projects they wanted to work on. But flat hierarchies can often mean unrealistic working hours and expectations because, hey, we are all equally responsible and not all roles are defined.

Sandeep Singh Agarwal, a start-up employee based in Bengaluru, was prescient about the Indian start-up ecosystem. 'The start-up that I joined didn't have an onboarding structure to align new employees. I was forwarded all the emails and tasks, and it felt like I was being bombarded with work without even understanding the product in depth. It was overwhelming,' he said. 'I have observed that there is a dearth of skill and competence when it comes to hiring for mid and senior level roles in the Indian start-up space.' Having interviewed for various roles in different start-ups, Agarwal believes the bar for performance and expectation is far above average, and that's why it is very difficult to get a good job in the Indian start-up ecosystem, especially at mid and senior levels.

Are Start-up Teams Like Families?

In India, most start-up teams aspire to be like a family. A side-effect of this is that there are clearly no boundaries to when bosses can reach their employees. It can be at any time of the day or night. Thanks to the plethora of messaging tools such as WhatsApp, there is no concept of personal space.

Pooja Sarkar, a dear friend and *Forbes* journalist, expressed this frustration in a tweet:[5]

FIG 5.2 The threat to work-life balance is real

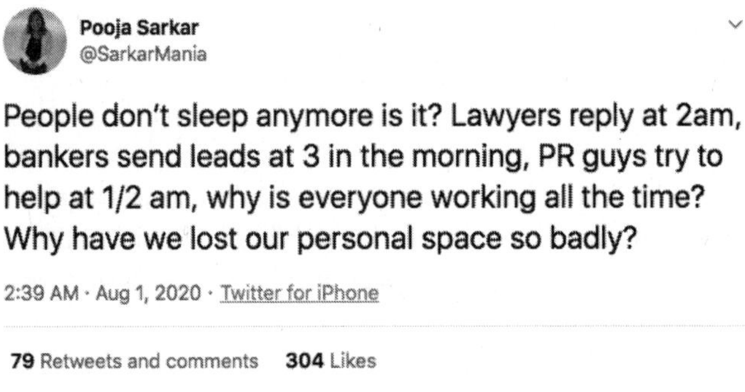
Pooja Sarkar
@SarkarMania

People don't sleep anymore is it? Lawyers reply at 2am, bankers send leads at 3 in the morning, PR guys try to help at 1/2 am, why is everyone working all the time? Why have we lost our personal space so badly?

2:39 AM · Aug 1, 2020 · Twitter for iPhone

79 Retweets and comments **304** Likes

Our passion to succeed and complete disregard for others' privacy have often led to burnout. We reply to our bosses at 10 pm because it is not just a professional relationship. We want to be available for the company and also want to impress our superiors. If I don't reply, someone else will, and then that person will be a more valued employee. Such thoughts have invariably crossed our minds when we don't respond to our bosses. A combination of FOMO and undue competitiveness has led us to a lifestyle where we never allow ourselves to switch off. What's more, doing so is considered unacceptable. There have been situations where employees are fired because they made themselves unavailable to respond to office emails beyond work hours. Within funded start-ups, the pressure is even higher.

However, globally, companies have different views on this. Bjorn Bakker, a European start-up founder, is an interesting mix of ambition and emotional intelligence.

Sipping his second cup of black coffee at 8.05 am at a quaint cafe in Berlin, he said to me,

> I think the analogy of the family in companies is very broken. What I understand from companies such as Netflix is they don't see each other as family. They treat each other as a sports team. This doesn't mean you don't have meaningful relationships with each other, but it does create a sort of different mindset. Sometimes what goes wrong with feel-good culture is that, let's say, if you have a brother and he goes to prison for whatever reason, you will still love him. Right? With a sports team, you probably won't love a teammate who goes to prison.

As far as I'm concerned, Bakker's family analogy would never work in the Indian context.

I think big sports teams have a brotherhood feeling among their members, the same feeling that the defence forces have inside a barrack. If somebody falls down, the others would pick her up, but they won't support unethical practices.

Founders Can't Avoid Being Narcissistic

Whether in India or the world, narcissism is much talked about in the tech world. Studies show that narcissistic business founders are loved by investors because they exude confidence. Apparently, some level of narcissism is desirable in a leader; it will make them believe in themselves regardless of what the world thinks about them. But the problem is that narcissists have a way of stepping out of line. That's where a line must be drawn between an acceptable level of narcissism and a disaster.

Professors Dean McFarlin and Paul Sweeney proposed six types of narcissistic leadership that can be detrimental to an organisation:[6]

- those who manipulate others to gain recognition, are good at using lies, mislead others, roar and use coercive tactics;
- narcissistic leaders who are impulsive, quirky and irritable;
- narcissistic leaders who place undue emphasis on image management;
- narcissistic leaders who lack management practices;
- narcissistic leaders who cannot truly understand their own abilities;
- narcissistic leadership that results in the failure of a succession plan.

These six types of harmful narcissistic leadership qualities basically summarise the negative effects of all narcissistic leadership. Two other researchers Chatterjee and Hambrick, through data analysis of listed companies in the IT industry, found that:

- narcissistic leadership is dynamically related to decision-making and the frequency and size of the merger;
- narcissistic leaders prefer to take courageous actions and attract more attention, leading to greater profits or losses;
- a narcissistic leader's company faces greater volatility.

There is no significant difference in performance. All the data Chatterjee et al. used are objective indicators, so this is the most persuasive research on the impact narcissistic leaders have on performance. This result seems to indicate that from a performance point of view, narcissistic leadership is not entirely negative.[7]

Insecurities and Narcissism Go Hand in Hand

A few years ago, an anonymous employee of a start-up wrote an article in the *Guardian*. It said,

> A startup founder's personality problems can manifest themselves in a variety of ways: pathological lying to interviewees and customers about the product; wildly contradictory decision-making; and the voicing of a million ridiculous ideas, every single one of which demands a response. (And because all the ideas are generally so hysterically unworkable, pointless or illegal – or all three – the response tends to be no, which of course means that you are the problem. Again.)
>
> Unable to prioritise, it didn't really matter what one particular startup boss I worked for was doing as long as he was doing something. Hunched over a computer, the boss in question would assault the keyboard as though his intended target was the desk beneath it. Read out of context you would be forgiven for thinking his emails had been written by somebody well into their third decade of being kept behind a false wall.
>
> Doing battle with a mind untethered from reality required superhuman patience and resilience. All of us became the de facto quality control department for his unfiltered thoughts. You either had to say no creatively, so that it sounded like yes, or no directly, which made you the problem, the blocker and merely the latest in a long line of obstructions to his grand vision. In reality, we were a team of firefighters led by an arsonist.[8]

The article did not imply that working in start-ups was bad or that start-ups couldn't be fun places to work. Rather, it implied that a lot of them operated completely at the mercy of the founders, the first few employees and the culture they had created for newer employees.

According to researchers Christopher N. Cascio, Sara H. Konrath and Emily B. Falk, narcissism and insecurities are deeply related. Narcissists have avoidant attachment styles, maintain distance in relationships and claim not to need others. However, they are especially sensitive to others' evaluations, needing positive-reflected appraisals to maintain their inflated self-views and showing extreme responses, for instance, aggression, when rejected.[9]

So how can an unhealthy level of narcissism and insecurity affect a business? While business founders have insecurities like any of us would, they don't or should not have the liberty to express them in front of their employees. Your employees are not your therapist or punching bag. Treating them as one is the stepping stone to disastrous work culture. What I have learned after a decade of meeting young business founders from across the globe and from being close friends with them is that their obsession with their companies makes them a person they are not.

Insecurities can be expressed in different ways:

Anger and short temperament: There are cultures where yelling and unpleasant meetings are normal. We all know that the boss is ill-tempered. To be scared of the big boss is normal in a patriarchal or matriarchal set-up. Fear is ever-present in these organisations. Even if people make mistakes, they would never admit it for fear of being reprimanded. I have been part of organisations where mistakes were never disclosed to the boss by employees. As a result, decisions were delayed and damage control was almost impossible because no one wanted to talk about the blunders. Professor Amy C. Edmondson wrote a book on creating a psychologically safe environment at work. In it, she talks about the culture of creating psychological safety in the workplace for learning, innovation and growth. 'Cheating and covering up are natural by-products of a top-down culture that does not accept "no" or "it can't be done" for an answer,' she says, 'But combining this culture with a belief that a brilliant strategy formulated in the past will hold indefinitely into the future becomes a certain recipe for failure.'[10]

Control freaks: These are bosses who are unwilling to relegate control to others because of the misplaced belief that subordinates will always make mistakes. This also comes from not being able to trust anyone except oneself.

Need for validation: Narcissistic bosses are wont to take undue credit for other people's work and not share success with others because their need for validation is greater than anyone else's in the company.

Some founders have one component of insecurity more than the other. While I have been extremely lucky to work with some of the best young founders, I have also had the experience of working with founders who bring a lot of personal baggage and ego while running the companies. Just like any relationship has red flags in the beginning, these traits are easy to spot. Once my founder-boss got angry with me because he thought I did not reply to his Slack message and demolished all my ideas in the meeting. Later, he apologises for his mistake. Most of these behaviours reveal shades of narcissism.

Bootstrapped or VC funded, burnout and depression are the sad realities of Indian start-ups. The wave of most new jobs created is being ruled by start-ups. One out of every five employees of India incorporated is suffering from workplace depression, says a new survey.[11] Medical experts blame it on the lack of support systems at both the workplace and in personal circles. How can business founders tackle their own mental health and that of their employees', and how can investors consider it as something as important as a return on investment?

6

No One Wants to Miss the India Story

India is now the most populous country in the world. But unlike China, which it has surpassed in 2023, over 50 per cent of India's population is under the age of twenty-five, which immediately gives India the demographic advantage. With over seven hundred million internet users – and that number is growing – it took no time for India to become a cradle of start-ups. In 2021, India had forty-four unicorns.[1] It's clearly the favourite among venture capitalists.

I witnessed this rise as a young start-up journalist in the country and eventually also witnessed shades of scepticism in Indian and international media about the start-up scene in India, but the future is bright.

What Works in India and What Went Wrong?

In March 2020, the *Economist* did a cover story on the start-up scene in India, which had a few takeaways. First, it said that India had eighty thousand start-ups. The country raised $10 billion in capital in 2019, up from $3.1 billion in 2012. These numbers put India's VC activity behind America ($114 bn) and China ($34 bn) but ahead of larger economies such as Germany and France.

Second, it highlighted the fact that the country has eighteen unlisted unicorns valued at more than $1 billion apiece. In 2021, India had forty-four unicorns, which was two more than the cumulative count of unicorns in the nine previous years.

The *Economist* story noted, 'Bright engineers and managers now aspire to work for them – or their VC backers – rather than settle for safe careers at a multinational, a bank or a state-run firm. Another 150-odd "soonicorns" may reach the $1 billion mark shortly.'

After talking about huge numbers, the *Economist* addressed the 800-pound gorilla in the room about the start-up scene in India: 'But their (unicorns) growth is limited in a country rich in people but poor in disposable income. And, like counterparts in the West, few of them make any money. The reasons – and justifications – are the same, too: heavy investments are necessary to acquire new customers and achieve scale.'

While there has been the landmark Flipkart–Walmart deal, it accounted for 80 per cent of the ten biggest exits in 2018, according to Bain Capital. Most exits in India have been secondary stake sales from one VC to another.

There might be doubts or scepticism, but no one wants to miss the India story despite the challenges. Even during the COVID-19 crisis in 2020, Sequoia's limited partnership (LP) invested another $1.3 billion in two new India funds. In August 2020, Lightspeed India Partners raised its new fund Lightspeed India Partners III with a commitment of $275 million from global institutional LPs.

Shailendra Singh, managing partner of Peak XV Partners (formerly Sequoia Capital India), wrote in a LinkedIn post:

> COVID-19 has brought us closer to embracing some hard truths. The start-up ecosystem in India and SEA has had a tumultuous journey over the last decade. During periods of exuberance, investors have rushed in to invest large amounts

> of capital into start-ups. This has, expectedly, resulted in short-term overfunding and hyper competition amongst start-ups. These periods have been followed by down cycles, cost cutting and negative sentiment. These cycles have enhanced start-up mortality and left many founders, investors and start-up employees scarred. Due to frequent cycles of intense competition, start-ups in our region have struggled to grow rapidly with good unit economics, often posting very high losses for the scale of business. This has prevented very large profitable technology businesses in our region from emerging. To add to these challenges, start-ups in India do not have the benefit of a regulatory framework that allows listing on foreign exchanges like Nasdaq. In this market context, most start-ups have chosen to remain private, and raising capital has become a proxy for success. We believe there is an opportunity to choose a different path. Our ecosystem has arrived at a fork in the road.

This was precisely the time most VCs and PE players started emphasising even more on unit economics and profitability.

India Needs Human Capital and Productivity

The argument of the *Economist* on low disposable income in India is deep-rooted. We can't afford what we want to buy; we don't produce what we consume. During the COVID-19 crisis, Prime Minister Narendra Modi announced Atmanirbhar Bharat, a measure to boost self-reliance in India.[2] Incentives were announced for India-made products and Indian start-ups, which sought to solve problems faced by India. How that has translated into a start-up boom is still up for debate.

Raju Vegesna, chief evangelist at Zoho, has a bone to pick with the way we are dealing with young talent in India:

> When you have a lot of young people graduating from college and when you see all of these people joining these various companies and moving abroad and trying to be productive there, you arrive at a question: why is it that we have a lot of young talent but we are not able to create world-class companies out of India to retain them? Then you have to look at some basic numbers: why is India a poor country? You have to ask the fundamental questions and some of it is not technology related, rather it is philosophical.

What India really needs is productivity. Productivity means having to produce something so that we can generate profit and have enough capacity to buy things. You cannot earn $200–$300 a year and try to buy a phone that costs $800. You have to produce thousands of dollars' worth of products before you can afford something. Sridhar Vembu and Raju Vegensa, who have built Zoho as a global technology company, have time and again spoken about the problem of productivity in India:

> As a start-up that was founded in India, we can create products or generate productivity out of India. And we cannot do this overnight; you have to do it over multiple decades and you need to build capital. Unfortunately, in today's world, for a lot of entrepreneurs, capital means money, that's the sad state today. Capital is not just money, and money is one form of capital. You've got to build the human form of capital, which is capital to learn how to create products.

In his 2011 blog, Vembu wrote,

> I am in business because I believe there is really only one solution. We need 25x more businesses, 25x more jobs, 25x more infrastructure before India could be considered a liveable country. I hope to live to see a day when one city, just one

> f**king city, in India will offer a world-class quality of life. Today, almost no city in India comes close to offering what would be considered an acceptable quality of life. That is why I wake up every day and go to work, because my dream is to create sufficient profits to directly fund the infrastructure we need to live a decent life.

Vembu recognises the conditions under which people work in the country – the roads and the infrastructure. People write code, support customers, teach and learn from each other, all under these conditions. The fact that we ship products under these conditions is a testimony to the resilience of the human spirit.

Vembu acknowledges that Indians are generally hard-working despite being forced to live under a broken system:

> Governments in India are famous for a singular lack of vision and imagination. In that picture, for example, you would think the local municipal body would be responsible for the civic infrastructure.
>
> We have ministries and departments for everything under the sun, from condoms to condiments, from rain forests to railways, from fisheries to fertilisers, from information technology to imaging satellites. Except that we don't focus on basics like roads, sanitation or drinking water, because, well, that would be too obvious and too sensible. Ronald Reagan's dictum 'Government is not the solution to our problems, government is the problem' applies with astonishing force and clarity in India. That is why I am a businessman.

Companies that build capital in the long term are not only able to help themselves and their employees but also the economy. In 2020, when the world was hit by the COVID-19 pandemic and everyone was struggling to survive, including VC-funded companies, Vembu put his money back into the economy. He tweeted that the donation was possible because of the company's focus on building human capital and reliance and support from customers.

FIG 6.1 Businesses donate millions of dollars in donation

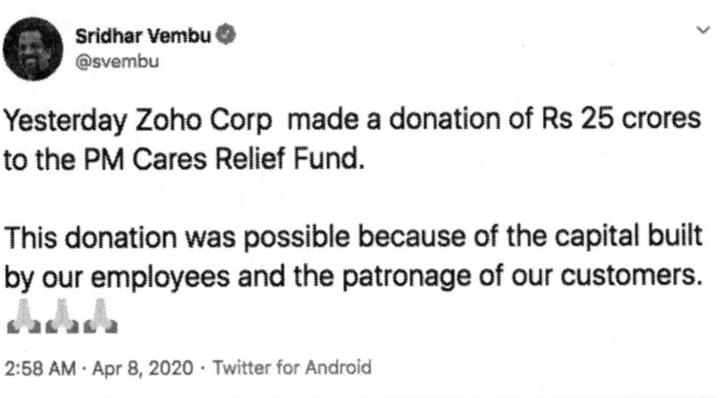

Sridhar Vembu
@svembu

Yesterday Zoho Corp made a donation of Rs 25 crores to the PM Cares Relief Fund.

This donation was possible because of the capital built by our employees and the patronage of our customers. 🙏🙏🙏

2:58 AM · Apr 8, 2020 · Twitter for Android

Build Products, More Products

According to Raju, back in 1996, nobody was aggressively creating products out of India. 'We decided we need to create that capital, the awareness, all of that. You need to build the product management capital; you need to build the design capital; you need to do some research and create a ton of things and build things up,' he said. 'So this is all non-financial capital that you've got to build to create a long-term company, and that is essentially what we started building back in the day.'

Raju compared the revenue per employee of an IT services company such as TCS and Wipro to a product company such as Apple:

> The average revenue per employee of IT companies like TCS or Wipro would be about $55,000, so it cannot pay more than $55,000 for any employee it hires. Now, if you do the same

> calculation for product companies, the numbers are going to be significantly high. Revenue per employee for Apple will probably come down to a couple of millions. Maybe even profit per employee is going to be about a million plus for all these companies. Product companies do significantly better than services companies.

According to Statista, in 2020, Apple ranked second with an annual revenue of almost $1.9 million per employee.

Vembu on the other hand highlighted the cascading effects of productivity. According to him, when an individual works hard and adds value to his labour, it rubs off on the entire community and the nation:

> When productivity goes up, you can pay a good salary to an employee. When you pay a good salary to an employee, they will take their savings and invest in something else, which will benefit another family, and that's how the quality of life of a community improves. So, how do we do that? How do we elevate the quality of life of a community? It's by improving productivity. If you make a lot of profit, then you'll create maybe another company that also does something similar, and you keep creating value and that will fundamentally benefit the entire community and, hopefully, eventually the country.

During the pandemic, even VCs started speaking a similar language. The shift went from scale to profits to building products. Shailendra Singh wrote in the blog and dedicated it to all such founders who are inspired to build legendary companies that can transform industries and outlive the founders and early investors:

> It's time to aspire for massively large and profitable companies. It's time to build more products that can compete globally

on quality, not just on price. We need more unique and innovative start-ups pursuing original ideas in addition to 'X of Y' business models. We need more examples of authentic leadership, improvements in gender diversity and inclusive, safe and nurturing work culture for our teams. In short, our ecosystem needs exemplary, enduring, lighthouse companies of the future, which can prosper for decades and be resilient across market cycles. We are at a fork in the road and everyone has a choice to make. From our vantage point, the future of our region will be shaped by those few founders who are resolutely committed to building enduring companies with unshakable foundations. It will take a handful of exceptional founders to show us the way, to shine the light for others to follow.

How to Build Capital Out of India

Talent is the least of India's problems. Some of the finest leaders of technology companies come from India. Pichai Sundararajan, also known as Sundar Pichai, is an Indian-American business executive. He is the CEO of Alphabet and its subsidiary Google. Satya Nadella, the Indian-origin chief executive officer of Microsoft, succeeded Steve Ballmer in 2014. Before becoming the CEO, he was the executive vice president of Microsoft's cloud and enterprise group, responsible for building and running the company's computing platforms. Both Pichai and Nadella have led their respective companies to market capitalisations of over $1 trillion since taking over.

But why is it that we cannot create Apple or Google out of India? According to Raju, despite our talent pool, we haven't even really tried it to be able to tell if we are capable of building an Apple or a Google out of India:

> You can! Just that you have to try first. All you know, you might fail, but without trying, you wouldn't even know whether you

> [will] succeed or fail. So, we sat on the mission of saying we'll try. We might just fall flat on our face a decade or two later, but that's fine. At least somebody has to try because everything else points to it; everything else says there is good talent in the country. We produce 1.2 million engineers every year; there is definitely talent out there, and there is vision. If we show them the good vision and start executing, eventually we can create a large company out of India and make a substantial impact in the community.

The founders of Zoho believe that building a company is a long-term game, and it is not common in today's world any more.

> We say Microsoft is successful and Windows 95 is the hit product of Microsoft. But Microsoft started around '77 or '78 right? The real success only came 20 years later. During this time, they were building that capital and expertise. They made mistakes and gained knowledge. Theirs is not an overnight success, they had to fight hard and work hard, build that capital to get to where they eventually ended up. And the same thing can be said with Apple or Google or a lot of these companies.

Why Do We Need Entrepreneurs That Create Value in the Long Term?

What did Japan do between nineteen sixties and nineteen ninety that made it an advanced economy today? What has changed since? How did companies such as Sony, Toyota, Nissan and Honda run for fifty or a hundred years? What is the culture and the fundamentals of such companies, and why is it that India doesn't have a lot of those companies? And how do we adopt those? How do we get that culture?

It's not like people get on an aeroplane, come to the US and suddenly become smart. Rather, they join companies that have figured out a way to make them productive and have an innovation culture. What is it that Western companies or, in some cases, Japanese companies have that Indian companies don't, and how do we bring those elements to raise productivity in India and create global companies out of India? The answer is simple. It is productivity.

How Is the Indian Start-up Ecosystem Perceived Globally?

There are two parts to this question. How is India perceived in emerging countries? And how is India perceived globally? Rajan Anandan, managing director of Sequoia Capital India (now called Peak XV Partners), said there are three large start-up ecosystems in the world: the US, China and India, in that order. After that you could include Israel and then possibly the UK, which used to be the hub of start-ups in Europe. In Asia, countries such as Indonesia, Singapore and Vietnam could be in the top twenty.

Talking about India, Anandan said, 'If you go back to 2010, the start-up ecosystem was virtually non-existent. You had literally a few hundred companies in the whole country and so on. I actually don't think of the Indian ecosystem any longer in an Asian context. It's a very relevant ecosystem and an important ecosystem in a global context today.'

Rajan's logic to look at India as an opportunity is simple. He said, 'If your start-up is sitting in France, Germany or the UK, India may not be relevant to you. If you're a large Silicon Valley–based technology company like Google, Facebook or Amazon, India is a must-win market. Google, Facebook and Amazon are giving absolutely everything they have to win these markets.'

According to Anandan,

> The way to think about India is that if you're a global tech company and if you have global ambitions to be, let's say, in the global internet space, there are 3.5 billion internet users in the world today, 500 million of them are in India. And if you go to 2025, that number will probably get to about 5 billion, and a billion of them will be in India, right? Billions of your consumers will be in India and around 1.3 billion in China. Half the global internet will be in China and India, and for most internet companies outside of China, China is not really addressable as of today, thanks to regulatory issues. Essentially, you can't really be a global internet company if you're not in India and if you are not winning India.

India Is a User Story and Not for Everyone

In the start-up world, if you don't understand your user, you are absolutely a wreck. And in a country like India, multiply its relevance by a hundred times more. Most global companies have had problems making a profit out of India, except the biggies. You need deep pockets and a risk appetite to survive here. It is a long-term and a volume game.

I vividly remember meeting John Flannery, CEO of GE India, in June 2011. At a time when strong India sales were lifting global sales and profit boats of many multinational companies such as PepsiCo, Coca-Cola, Huawei and Boeing, GE botched its chances when it could have leveraged its century-old presence in India and acted as its global growth engine. GE's India operations contributed just 1.2 per cent to its $157 billion sales annually. GE India sales constantly missed its revenue targets. This is when the market for its core businesses – power equipment, aircraft engines, medical devices and finance – was booming. Being optimistic, Flannery had told me, 'Our whole learning in India has been how to become a really local company. The faster we do it, the more successful we will be. And we will also face our competitors better. In addition, we are trying to learn from experiences here and apply them in other markets like Indonesia and China.'

Alex Osterwalder, founder of Strategyzer and Business Model Canvas, had a different opinion:

> I can tell you why GE doesn't succeed in markets like India. Because they look at it as an execution problem, but it's not an execution problem. It's actually a search problem. Search for a value proposition that creates value for that specific customer segment embedded in a business model that can profitably scale. This will vary from one market to another, and then maybe you have one that could work in several markets that you'll find from the details. But you don't know in advance what's going to work so you actually have to admit you don't know. Companies like GE don't admit they don't know. They're getting humbler now because they can't innovate, 90 per cent of the companies don't know how to innovate. Now they're starting to be humble because it's basically two things you need to do constantly: design and shape your ideas.

If you are a GE or a big corporation, you will have a portfolio of business models, and you can decide simultaneously which one works for you and which does not. If you're a start-up, you probably have one business model. You will have to figure out how to make it work. There are questions that are specific to start-ups and large companies; there are also questions specific to emerging markets. You need to know your place in this Venn diagram of essential versus luxury products: audience, country of operation and price point. People don't ask those questions enough. I don't think the business understanding is enough for people to ask these basic but fundamental questions, especially for an emerging market.

India is a user story, and it will become more and more important as a user story as disposable incomes increase. Monetisation can happen in many different ways. If you're a consumer internet company, you can make money in three ways: consumers can pay you on platforms such as Netflix, you can make money through advertising on, say, Google or you can make money through e-commerce platforms such as Flipkart and Amazon.

According to Anandan, companies that want to invest in India need strategic planning:

> If your ambition is not to be a leading global company that is massively relevant in 2030, India may not be for you, which is perfectly fine. India is not for everyone. You have to come here with a long-term perspective. You have to come here with serious intent. This is one of the most strategic markets for the five FAANG (Facebook, Apple, Amazon, Netflix and Google). And these are the most successful technology companies on the planet.

India is large and complex. It's massively scaleable. It's hypercompetitive. This is where the best in the world compete to win. It's not a fun place to be if you don't have high ambitions.

NOTES

FOREWORD

1 https://www.start-upindia.gov.in/content/sih/en/international/go-to-market-guide/indian-start-up-ecosystem.html (accessed on 5 May 2022)

CHAPTER 1: DO START-UPS NEED JUST MONEY OR VC MONEY?

1 Anthony Isola, 'In Wealth-Building, Focus on the Playing Field not the Scoreboard,' The Christian Science Monitor, 27 August 2015, https://www.csmonitor.com/Business/Saving-Money/2015/0827/In-wealth-building-focus-on-the-playing-field-not-the-scoreboard#:~:text=As%20Warren%20Buffett%20once%20said,of%20success%20will%20increase%20immensely
2 Rashi Varshney, 'How Wingify Bootstrapped and Built a Profitable Company Out of India,' YourStory, 30 August 2020, https://yourstory.com/2020/08/how-wingify-bootstrapped-and-built-a-profitable-co/amp
3 Shradha Sharma, 'Divyank Turakhia Writes to Media.net Staff, Says He Is Stepping Down as CEO,' YourStory, 16 October 2018, https://yourstory.com/2018/10/divyank-turakhia-media-net-staff-stepping-down-ceo/amp
4 David Cox, 'The Complete Zerodha Review 2023,' CryptoNewZ, 3 May 2023, https://www.cryptonewsz.com/forex-brokers/zerodha-review/ (accessed on 29 May 2023)
5 'Private Equity vs. Venture Capital: What's the Difference?' Investopedia, https://www.investopedia.com/ask/answers/020415/what-difference-between-private-equity-and-venture-capital.asp#:~:text=Private%20equity%20is%20capital%20invested,potential%20for%20long%2Dterm%20growth (accessed on 27 January 2022)
6 'Venture Capital: What Is VC and How Does It Work?' Investopedia, https://www.investopedia.com/terms/v/venturecapital.asp (accessed on 31 May 2022)

7 'Initial Public Offering (IPO): What It Is and How It Works,' Investopedia, https://www.investopedia.com/terms/i/ipo.asp (accessed on 28 June 2022)

8 https://www.clearlightpartners.com/private-equity-vs-venture-capital/

9 Maulik Vyas and Sneha Shah, 'Catwalk in Talks to Sell 26% to IVFA for Rs 100 Crore,' *Economic Times*, 1 November 2012, https://economictimes.indiatimes.com/industry/cons-products/fashion-/-cosmetics-/-jewellery/catwalk-in-talks-to-sell-26-pc-to-ivfa-for-rs-100-crore/articleshow/17044714.cms?from=mdr

10 Debjyoti Roy, 'Women's Footwear Maker Catwalk Gets Strategic Investor,' VCCircle, 21 March 2016, https://www.vccircle.com/exclusive-womens-footwear-maker-catwalk-gets-strategic-investor (accessed on 29 March 2023)

11 Shrutika Verma and Mihir Dalal, 'Snapdeal's Kunal Bahl Admits to Mistakes, Founders to Forego Salary,' *Mint*, https://www.livemint.com/Companies/gaAaSkxWZE4Ri45GiuBHkN/Snapdeals-Kunal-Bahl-admits-to-mistakes-to-take-100-salar.html (accessed on 23 February 2017)

12 https://en.wikipedia.org/wiki/Info_Edge (accessed on 29 May 2023)

13 Brian Womack, 'After Relocation from California, Dallas Company Gets Backing from Yelp CEO, Other Tech Leaders,' *Dallas Business Journal*, 9 December 2020, https://www.bizjournals.com/dallas/news/2020/12/09/signeasy-yelp-ceo.html

CHAPTER 2: ACQUIRING CUSTOMERS IN A DATA-DRIVEN AGE IN INDIA

1 Catherine Tucker and Nico Neumann, 'Buying Consumer Data? Tread Carefully,' *Harvard Business Review*, 1 May 2020, https://hbr.org/2020/05/buying-consumer-data-tread-carefully

2 Nilesh Christopher, 'IT Outsourcing Firm GlobalLogic Has Crossed $550 Million in Revenues,' *Economic Times*, 20 February 2018, https://economictimes.indiatimes.com/tech/ites/it-outsourcing-firm-globallogic-has-crossed-550-million-in-revenues/articleshow/62992546.cms?from=mdr

3 https://www.linkedin.com/in/petercharrison/details/experience/

4 Paras Chopra (@paraschopra), Twitter, 9 June 2020, 5:57 pm, https://twitter.com/paraschopra/status/1270332745416351744
5 Eric Jorgenson, 'Building Start-ups,' Almanack of Naval Ravikant, https://www.navalmanack.com/secret-sections/building-start-ups
6 Biswarup Gooptu and Gulveen Aulakh, 'Uber to Integrate Paytm's Digital Wallet into Its Payment System,' *Economic Times*, 13 November 2014, https://economictimes.indiatimes.com/small-biz/start-ups/uber-to-integrate-paytms-digital-wallet-into-its-payment-system/articleshow/45129888.cms?from=mdr
7 Chris Wright, 'How Paytm Went Big on Indian Demonetisation,' *Euromoney*, 29 November 2017, https://www.euromoney.com/article/b15ts6qpxvj51d/how-paytm-went-big-on-indian-demonetization
8 Neha Alawadhi, 'Paytm Payments Bank Registers Over 970 Million Transactions in March 2021,' *Business Standard*, 13 April 2021, https://www.business-standard.com/article/companies/paytm-payments-bank-registers-over-970-million-transactions-in-march-2021-121041300049_1.html
9 Subrata Panda, 'UPI Signs off 2021 on a high: Dec transaction value crosses Rs 8 trillion,' *Business Standard*, 3 January 2022, https://www.business-standard.com/article/finance/upi-ends-calendar-year-2021-with-record-high-transactions-in-dec-122010100411_1.html
10 Shweta Modgil, 'The Date Story: How TrulyMadly Dated Digital Media to Drive More Sign Ups,' Inc42, 10 February 2016, https://inc42.com/resources/trulymadly-digital-media/
11 TrulyMadly @thetrulymadly, Twitter, 22 October 2015, 11:27 am, https://mobile.twitter.com/thetrulymadly/status/657126147617001472
12 Sridhar Vembu, 'They Acquire, Acquire, Acquire While We Build, Build, Build,' Zoho Blog, 4 June 2013, https://www.zoho.com/blog/general/they-acquire-acquire-acquire-while-we-build-build-build.html
13 Sindhu Hariharan, 'SaaS Company Zoho Hits $1 Billion in Revenue,' *Times of India*, 9 November 2022, https://timesofindia.indiatimes.com/business/india-business/saas-company-zoho-hits-1-billion-in-revenue/articleshow/95390046.cms

14 Yuvraj Malik, 'Paytm Acquires Nearbuy and Little, to Merge Both,' *Mint*, 7 December 2017, https://www.livemint.com/Companies/KTsJ4Szt1ORbpRVMDHMCwL/Paytm-acquires-Nearbuy-and-Little-to-merge-both.html

CHAPTER 3: DO YOU WANT INDIANS TO PAY FOR YOUR PRODUCT?

1 'How to Find the Right Financial Partner,' *Mint*, 2 March 2019, https://www.livemint.com/money/personal-finance/how-to-find-the-right-financial-planner-1551093751169.html
2 Disha Sanghvi, 'Most Indians in Middle, High Income Groups Save for Retirement, Says Report,' *Mint*, 23 April 2019, https://www.livemint.com/money/personal-finance/most-indians-in-middle-high-income-groups-save-for-retirement-says-report-1556024495227.html
3 Erin Griffith, 'These 50 Start-Ups May Be the Next "Unicorns",' *New York Times*, 10 February 2019, https://www.nytimes.com/2019/02/10/technology/these-50-start-ups-may-be-the-next-unicorns.html
4 Paras Chopra, 'Why You Shouldn't Set Prices Based on Value Created,' Inverted Passion, 25 December 2017, https://invertedpassion.com/why-you-shouldnt-set-prices-based-on-value-created/

CHAPTER 4: IS THERE AN IDEAL BUSINESS MODEL?

1 Wingify, 'VWO,' 28 February 2022, https://vwo.com/
2 Wingify, 'Bring Back Lost Visitors At 4x The Conversion Rate of Email,' 2022, https://vwo.com/engage/?ref=pc
3 Paras Chopra, 'Why many B2C Start-ups Pivot to B2B,' Inverted Passion, 9 January 2018, https://invertedpassion.com/why-many-b2c-start-ups-pivot-to-b2b/
4 'What the Walmart-Flipkart Deal Means for Indian E-commerce, Consumers and Amazon,' BQ Prime, 9 May 2018, https://www.bqprime.com/business/what-the-walmart-flipkart-deal-means-for-indian-e-commerce-amazon-and-consumers (accessed on 29 May 2023)
5 Adi Narayan, 'Why Infibeam Isn't Going the Flipkart Way,' *Mint*, 8 July 2015, https://www.livemint.com/Industry/9BQR05dfNVoFpreI07UeJK/Why-Infibeam-isnt-going-the-Flipkart-way.html

6 Todd Bishop, 'Amazon Web Services posts record $13.5B in *profits* for 2020 in Andy Jassy's AWS swan song,' *Geek Wire*, 2 February 2021, https://www.geekwire.com/2021/amazon-web-services-posts-record-13-5b-profits-2020-andy-jassys-aws-swan-song/
7 Felix Richter, 'Amazon Leads $200-Billion Cloud Market,' *Statista*, 2 August 2022, https://www.statista.com/chart/18819/worldwide-market-share-of-leading-cloud-infrastructure-service-providers/
8 Ajeet Khurana, 'E-Commerce Basics,' *The Balance*, 26 June 2019, https://www.thebalancemoney.com/let-s-ask-the-basic-question-what-is-ecommerce-1141599
9 Grady Mcgregor, 'Apple Finally Starts Selling Directly to Customers in the World's Fastest-Growing Smartphone Market,' *Fortune*, 23 September 2020, https://fortune.com/2020/09/23/apple-online-store-india-opening-launch/

CHAPTER 5: NARCISSISM, DEPRESSION AND BURNOUT IN THE INDIAN START-UP ECOSYSTEM

1 Rachit Gupta (@_Rachit_Gupta_), Twitter, 7 June 2020, 5:30 pm, https://twitter.com/_Rachit_Gupta_/status/1269652986604601344
2 Sanchita Dash, 'This Indian Entrepreneur Started Going to Therapy and Recommends It to Start-up Founders to Survive the "Near Death" Moments in Business,' Business Insider, 13 July 2020, https://www.businessinsider.in/business/start-ups/news/therapy-and-mental-health-is-important-for-start-up-founders-to-survive-the-near-death-moments-in-business/articleshow/76931948.cms
3 Itika Sharma Punit and Sushma U.N., '"It's a Sweatshop": The Ugly Truth behind Working at an Indian Start-up,' Quartz India, 27 August 2018, https://qz.com/india/1222311/the-dark-underbelly-of-indias-glamourous-start-up-ecosystem/
4 Leroy Leo, 'OYO, CureFit and TapChief Top Start-ups to Work for in LinkedIn's List,' *Mint*, 4 September 2019, https://www.livemint.com/companies/start-ups/oyo-curefit-tapchief-top-start-ups-to-work-for-in-linkedin-s-list-1567598507195.html

5 Pooja Sarkar (@SarkarMania), Twitter, 1 August 2020, 6:09am, https://twitter.com/SarkarMania/status/1289360161602068481?s=20
7 Dean B. McFarlin and Paul D. Sweeney. *House of Mirrors: The Untold Truth about Narcissistic Leaders and How to Survive Them* (United States: Kogan Page Business Books, 2000).
8 Arijit Chatterjee and Donald Hambrick, 'It's All about Me: Narcissistic Chief Executive Officers and Their Effects on Company Strategy and Performance,' *Administrative Science Quarterly* 52, (2007) 351–386, DOI: 10.2189/asqu.52.3.351
9 Anonymous, 'The Secret Life of a Start-up Employee: It's Like Being a Firefighter Led by an Arsonist,' *The Guardian*, 26 September 2016, https://www.theguardian.com/commentisfree/2016/sep/26/secret-life-start-up-employee-rudderless-founded-by-capricious-narcissists
10 Christopher Cascio et al., 'Narcissists Social Pain Seen Only in the Brain,' *Social Cognitive and Affective Neuroscience* 10, no. 3, March 2015: 335–341, DOI: 10.1093/scan/nsu072
11 Amy C. Edmondson, 'The Fearless Organization: Creating Psychological Safety in the Workplace for Learning, Innovation, and Growth' (Hoboken, NJ: John Wiley & Sons, 2018).
12 Prachi Verma, 'Workplace Depression Taking a Toll on India Inc. Employees,' *The Economic Times*, 22 January 2019, https://economictimes.indiatimes.com/jobs/workplace-depression-taking-a-toll-on-india-inc-employees/articleshow/67633549.cms?from=mdr

CHAPTER 6: NO ONE WANTS TO MISS THE INDIA STORY

1 Howindialives.com, 'How India's Unicorns Galloped into 2022, in Charts,' *Mint*, 11 January 2022, https://www.livemint.com/companies/start-ups/the-many-advances-made-by-indian-unicorns-in-2021-11641794734159.html
2 PIB, 'PM Gives a Clarion Call for Atmanirbhar Bharat,' Prime Minister's Office, 12 May 2020, https://pib.gov.in/PressReleasePage.aspx?PRID=1623391

REFERENCES

Anonymous. 'The Secret Life of a Start-up Employee: It's Like Being a Firefighter Led by an Arsonist.' *The Guardian*, 26 September 2016.

BFSI Network. 'CCD Co-founder Who Went Missing Suggests Financial Woes in Letter to Board of Directors.' *The Banking and Finance Post*, 30 July 2019.

Biswarup, G. and Aulakh Gulveen. 'Uber to Integrate Paytm's Digital Wallet into Its Payment System.' *The Economic Times*, 13 November 2014.

Cascio, N. Christopher, Konrath, S.H. and Emily B. Falk. 'Narcissists Social Pain Seen Only in the Brain.' *Social Cognitive and Affective Neuroscience* 10, no. 3 (March 2015): 335–341, DOI: 10.1093/scan/nsu072.

Chatterjee, Arijit and Donald Hambrick. 'It's All About Me: Narcissistic Chief Executive Officers and Their Effects on Company Strategy and Performance.' *Administrative Science Quarterly* 52 (2007): 351–386, DOI: 10.2189/asqu.52.3.351.

Chopra, Paras. 'Why Many B2C Start-ups Pivot to B2B.' Inverted Passion, 9 January 2018.

————. 'Why You Shouldn't Set Prices Based on Value Created.' Inverted Passion, 25 December 2017.

Christopher, Nilesh. 'IT Outsourcing Firm GlobalLogic Has Crossed $550 Million in Revenues.' *The Economic Times*, 20 February 2018.

Croswell, Alexis. 'Why Do Founders Have Big Egos?' Torch, 15 August 2019.

Dash, Sanchita. 'This Indian Entrepreneur Started Going to Therapy and Recommends It to Start-up Founders to Survive the "Near Death" Moments in Business.' Business Insider, 13 July 2020.

Edmondson, Amy C., *The Fearless Organisation: Creating Psychological Safety in the Workplace for Learning, Innovation, and Growth* (Hoboken, NJ: John Wiley and Sons, 2018).

Griffith, Erin. 'These 50 Start-Ups May Be the Next "Unicorns".' *The New York Times*, 10 February 2019.

Howindialives. 'How India's Unicorns Galloped into 2022, in Charts.' *Mint*, 11 January 2022.

Investopedia. 'Initial Public Offering (IPO): What It Is and How It Works.' Accessed on 28 June 2022.

————. 'Private Equity vs. Venture Capital: What's the Difference?' Accessed on 27 January 2022.

————. 'Venture Capital: What Is VC and How Does It Work?' Accessed on 31 May 2022.

Jorgenson, Eric. 'Building Start-ups.' Navalmanack.

Khurana, Ajeet. 'E-commerce Basics.' The Balance, 26 June 2019.

Leroy, Leo. 'OYO, CureFit and TapChief Top Start-ups to Work for in LinkedIn's List.' *Mint*, 4 September 2019.

Malik, Yuvraj. 'Paytm Acquires Nearbuy and Little, to Merge Both.' *Mint*, 7 December 2017.

McFarlin, Dean B. and Paul D. Sweeney. *House of Mirrors: The Untold Truth About Narcissistic Leaders and How to Survive Them* (United States: Kogan Page Business Books, 2000).

Mcgregor, Grady. 'Apple Finally Starts Selling Directly to Customers in the World's Fastest-Growing Smartphone Market.' *Fortune*, 23 September 2020.

Modgil, Shweta. 'The Date Story: How TrulyMadly Dated Digital Media to Drive More Sign Ups.' Inc 42, 10 February 2016.

Narayan, Adi. 'Why Infibeam Isn't Going the Flipkart Way.' *Mint*, 8 July 2015.

Neha, Alawadhi. 'Paytm Payments Bank Registers Over 970 Million Transactions in March 2021.' *Business Standard*, 13 April 2021.

Panda, Subrata. 'UPI Signs Off 2021 on a High: Dec Transaction Value Crosses Rs 8 Trillion.' *Business Standard*, 3 January 2022.

PIB. 'PM Gives a Clarion Call for Atmanirbhar Bharat.' Prime Minister's Office, 12 May 2020.

Richter, Felix. 'Amazon Leads $200-Billion Cloud Market.' Statista, 2 August 2022.

Sanghvi, Disha. 'Most Indians in Middle, High Income Groups Save for Retirement, Says Report.' *Mint*, 23 April 2019.

Sharma, Punit Itika and Sushma U.N., '"It's a Sweatshop": The Ugly Truth Behind Working at an Indian Start-up.' Quartz India, 27 August 2018.

Sharma, Shradha. 'Divyank Turakhia Writes to Media.net Staff, Says He Is Stepping Down as CEO.' YourStory, 16 October 2018.

Sophie, Aubrey. 'Could a Hidden "Bliss Point" be Threatening Your Health Goals?' *The Sydney Morning Herald*, 13 July 2020.

Staff Writer. 'How to Find the Right Financial Partner.' *Mint*, 2 March 2019.

Todd, Bishop. 'Amazon Web Services Posts Record $13.5B in "Profits" for 2020 in Andy Jassy's AWS Swan Song.' GeekWire, 2 February 2021.

Tucker, Catherine and Nico Neumann. 'Buying Consumer Data? Tread Carefully.' *Harvard Business Review*, 1 May 2020.

Varshney, Rashi. 'How Wingify Bootstrapped and Built a Profitable Company Out of India.' YourStory, 30 August 2020.

Vembu, Sridhar. 'They Acquire, Acquire, Acquire While We Build, Build, Build.' Zoho Blog, 4 June 2013.

Verma, Prachi. 'Workplace Depression Taking a Toll on India Inc. Employees.' *The Economic Times*, 22 January 2019.

Verma, Shrutika and Dalal Mihir. 'Snapdeal's Kunal Bahl Admits to Mistakes, Founders to Forego Salary.' *Mint*, 23 February 2017.

Vyas, Maulik and Sneha Shah. 'Catwalk in Talks to Sell 26 pc to IVFA for Rs 100 Crore.' *The Economic Times*, 1 November 2012.

Wingify. 'VWO.' 28 February 2022.

————. 'Bring Back Lost Visitors At 4x The Conversion Rate of Email.' 2022.

Womack, Brian. 'After Relocation from California, Dallas Company Gets Backing from Yelp CEO, Other Tech Leaders.' *Dallas Business Journal*, 9 December 2020.

Wright, Chris. 'How Paytm Went Big on Indian Demonetisation.' Euromoney, 29 November 2017.

INDEX